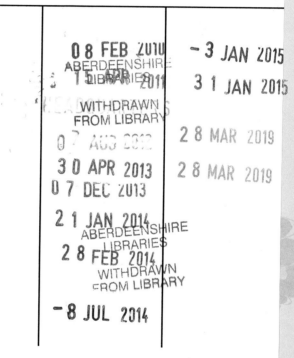

A GUIDE TO THE
GARDEN BIRDS
OF BRITAIN AND NORTHERN EUROPE
Dave Farrow

CARLTON
BOOKS

This edition published in 2009 by
Carlton Books Ltd
20 Mortimer Street
London
W1T 3JW

A CIP catalogue for this book is available from the British Library.

ISBN: 978 1 84442 032 2

Senior Editor: Gareth Jones
Copy Editor: James Parry
Senior Art Editor: Gülen Shevki-Taylor
Designer: Zoë Dissell
Artists: Brin Edwards, Mike Langman
Production: Lisa French

Printed in China

PREVIOUS PAGE: GREAT TIT (SEE PAGE 142)
BELOW: FIELDFARES & BLACKBIRD (SEE PAGES 112 AND 110)

Contents

ROBIN
*ERITHACUS
RUBECULA*

SWALLOW
HIRUNDO RUSTICA

Avian Topography

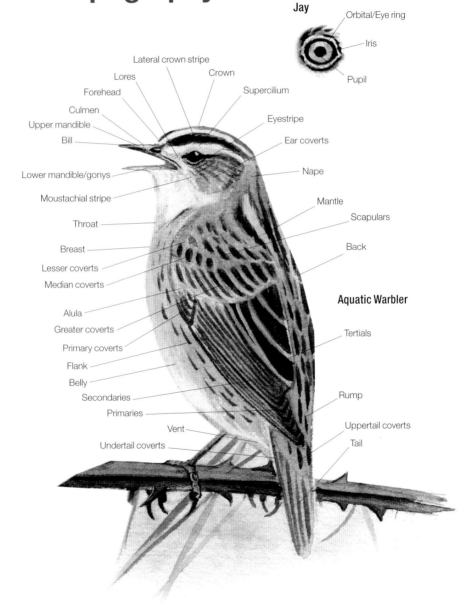

Jay

Orbital/Eye ring

Iris

Pupil

Lateral crown stripe

Crown

Lores

Supercilium

Forehead

Eyestripe

Culmen

Upper mandible

Ear coverts

Bill

Lower mandible/gonys

Nape

Moustachial stripe

Mantle

Throat

Scapulars

Breast

Back

Lesser coverts

Median coverts

Aquatic Warbler

Alula

Greater coverts

Tertials

Primary coverts

Flank

Belly

Secondaries

Rump

Primaries

Vent

Uppertail coverts

Undertail coverts

Tail

Introduction

Watching birds in the garden has often been the starting point for many of us who have since gone on to enjoy a lifelong interest in birds, and in wildlife generally. One day, either at a young age or perhaps later in life, you will notice a bird in your garden. You become transfixed by its beauty, fascinated by what it is doing, or simply curious because you have never noticed it before. This can be the first step on a long and very enjoyable, journey!

A garden can be considered to be one's own personal little patch of countryside, and so the birds seen in it assume a special importance. Aside from

TAWNY OWL
STRIX ALUCO

the feeling of 'ownership', the ease of observation and the confiding nature of birds in this often intimate environment provide a perfect introduction to the avian world. Garden birds are usually watched from within the house, and because the observer is frequently hidden from their view, they generally behave in a more confiding fashion than is usual in the presence of people, and often at very close range. This is how many of us start watching birds, and even for those who have had the opportunity to go birding in exotic parts of the world, the birds in the garden of one's own home will always have a special quality that is difficult to match.

It does not matter where your garden is, or how large it is. You will still find birds to watch, even in the most urban of areas. As more than 80 per cent of people in Britain live in cities and towns, this is where many take their first steps into the wonderful world of watching birds. Wherever you are, this book is intended as a companion guide to help you get the most out of garden birding. The various sections are designed to help you become a better garden birdwatcher, from developing your recognition skills to creating new habitats for birds in your garden. There are detailed accounts for 92 different bird species, as well as advice on which plants are best for birds, what food to put out, and how to provide bird-friendly features such as ponds and nest boxes. While you can never be sure which birds will turn up in your garden and when, one thing is guaranteed – that watching birds will give you many hours of pleasure and that your own garden is one of the best places to start. Good luck!

Watching Garden Birds

A remarkable number of people begin watching birds from their kitchen window, perhaps while standing at the sink! This will probably be the primary vantage point in the house for many, but from whatever point you look out, you need a clear view of the garden in order to observe the birds out there. A large window, particularly if it is in a patio door style with glass to the ground, is ideal, and upstairs windows can give an even greater view if the window arrangements allow easy and comfortable viewing. Once you know where your best vantage point is, then you can perhaps arrange your garden to suit you, the viewer. Trim back those overhanging branches so that you have a clear view of what is going on, and if you are feeding birds or putting out water, then make sure that you can see it, and the birds that will come to it. For much of the time, feeding birds is not a purely altruistic pastime – if you put food out, it is often to attract birds so that you can watch them from the comfort of your own home!

Of course, a garden is not just for looking at. It is your own patch of land in which to sit, relax, and grow flowers, other plants and vegetables, as well as for more boisterous activities such as children playing! Sitting quietly and relaxing in your garden will encourage avian visitors to do likewise. Many birds become quite confiding once they have got used to you and worked out that you are not a threat. You will also have a much broader field of view from an outdoor position, and be able to see 360 degrees around and up into the sky. It is a good idea to try and learn some of the commoner bird calls, as even a little knowledge will enable you to anticipate which species are present, even before they show themselves, a skill that will

NUTHATCH
SITTA EUROPAEA

greatly increase the number of birds you can find while you are outdoors.

The next step is to acquire some binoculars. It is not necessary to spend a large amount of money on these, but be warned – once you become used to good optics there is no going back! As long as they are bright and sharp enough to look through, so you avoid eyestrain and can see clearly through window glass, the magnification is not absolutely critical (7x or 8x will be perfectly adequate). There are many binocular retailers these days, and it is best to visit one of these and try out a few different pairs. Choose a pair that is easy to hold and comfortable for your eyes, bearing in mind that potentially you will be spending a lot of time looking through them and so they need to feel 'right'. Avoid high magnification binoculars (anything over 10x), unless you have some kind of clamp or tripod with which to keep them steady, as otherwise the image will be very shaky. A telescope is only useful if your garden is large or you have a good view over a wider sweep of habitat, such as fields, woods, or even the sea if you are lucky enough to live in a coastal location. Always remember to take good care of your binoculars. You can leave them on the windowsill by your vantage point so that they are always ready, but remember to cover the eyecups so they do not get dirty or damaged.

Try and keep notes, and write down anything of interest. This does not have to be in a very formal or structured manner – I keep an old exercise book on the windowsill, in which I scribble down any thing of interest (not just birds), plus the date. From such notes you can build up a record of sightings that can be referred to, year on year. However, as the garden birdwatcher is in the relaxed comfort of

BLUE TIT
CYANISTES CAERULEUS

their own home, a little discipline is required to write things down immediately, as otherwise it is all too easy to forget or get confused!

Once you start keeping notes, you will begin to build up a garden list. You will probably be surprised at the number of species you can record in your garden. Once you *really* start a garden list, you might have to define the parameters of your 'garden'. In fact, garden birding does not mean watching the area just within the four fences or hedges surrounding the plot – you can record anything flying over, birds heard calling overhead at night, and indeed anything that is visible from the house, front and back! As you build up a notebook of records, you can keep track of the seasons through your observations, noting the dates when summer and winter visitors first and last appear, as well as the activities of any birds that are nesting.

The garden is the perfect place to observe bird behaviour. It presents a mini-showcase, a focused area of wildlife action that coincides conveniently with your own comfort zone. As you begin to observe the birds in your garden, you will notice how some species prefer different parts of the garden. For example, Blackbirds and Robins feed primarily on the ground, whilst Blue Tits forage for caterpillars on the underside of the leaves, and Starlings loiter in gangs, often perched in trees or on rooftops, looking out for feeding opportunities. You will begin to observe the daily routines of birds, noticing how certain species only visit the garden in the early morning before disappearing elsewhere, while some are present throughout the day and yet others only become visible once food is put out. You will notice great changes through the seasons, from the busy flush of spring, when the garden may be alive with birdsong, through the quieter torpid months of summer, when many birds mysteriously disappear, to the mellow months of autumn, when migratory species are busy preparing to head south, and finally to the winter months, when some species become more obvious and garden feeding stations are at their busiest.

Spring is arguably the most exciting period, with lengthening days and warmer weather spurring on the reproduction race. Birds will start singing to attract a mate and defend a territory, and associated behaviour – such as the courtship of prospective breeding partners and conflict between rival males – can be observed in the garden on a daily basis. Nesting soon follows, and birds can be observed gathering material and building their nests, a busy period that is followed by a lull whilst incubation takes place. Next comes the incessant activity of feeding the young in the nest, followed by the youngsters fledging and then accompanying their parents until they are developed enough to be independent.

This latter period stretches into the summer months, and when all is done, birds disperse more widely. Adults may become more elusive as they quietly undergo a post-breeding moult, and summer can therefore be a quiet season in the garden, with the early mornings being the busiest time for bird activity. The later summer can be good for oddities, however, as less common species turn up in unlikely locations, either as part of a post-breeding dispersal or the early southward migration of birds from further north.

By autumn, familiar garden birds are setting up winter-feeding territories and migration is in full

DUNNOCK *PRUNELLA MODULARIS*

swing, with vast numbers of birds moving around the country and across the wider region. This is also a good time to see unusual birds, particularly in coastal gardens or those on an avian flyway, with flocks of birds such as Lapwings and Skylarks often passing overhead. At this time of year it is also worth carefully checking berry-carrying shrubs, as birds such as thrushes and Blackcaps (and even Waxwings) will be busy stripping them of their fruit.

The short days of winter mean that birds have only a few hours to secure enough food to fuel them through the long cold nights, and gardens are often alive with activity at this time. Spells of very cold weather, particularly in the late winter when natural food is usually in short supply, are a good time to see unusual birds in the garden, lured by the availability of food there. Typical winter visitors are birds such as Bramblings and Redwings, or species normally found in the arable country surrounding our towns and cities, such as Yellowhammers or Tree Sparrows.

Garden Habitats and Environment

The habitats in your garden will largely determine which birds and other wildlife occur there. From the simplest urban plot to a lush verdant tangle of vegetation within a larger wilderness, you will be able to see birds. There is, however, a sliding scale of bird diversity that runs in tandem with the general biodiversity of your garden. The more attractive a garden is in terms of plants and invertebrates, the greater the number and variety of birds to be found there.

Birds require four basic components: food, water, shelter and nesting sites. If you want to see more birds in your garden, then you should consider taking steps to increase its attractiveness to them by providing more opportunities for these core essentials. Feeding is dealt with in a separate section (see pages 20–23), so at this point we will look at habitats and 'wildlife gardening', and at a few simple measures with which to enhance your very own personal wildlife-viewing area.

The bird species found in your garden will vary according to the part of the country in which you live. While the species included in this book are meant to represent a reasonably comprehensive range of the birds likely to be encountered in a garden, some inner-city gardens will just not be large or diverse enough to attract more than the basic range of species. However, many people live in suburbs, where gardens are generally larger and the number of visiting bird species rises dramatically. Gardens located in a rural village or the open countryside, adjacent to areas of rich wildlife habitat or simply close to the coast, will attract even more species, including some that may well be in addition to those covered in this book.

The following list of 17 species can be considered the 'base layer' of birds likely to be seen in, and from, a typical urban garden:

- **Black-headed Gull**
- **Collared Dove**
- **Woodpigeon**
- **Feral Pigeon**
- **Swift**
- **Carrion Crow**
- **Magpie**
- **Starling**
- **Blackbird**
- **Wren**
- **Blue Tit**
- **Great Tit**
- **Robin**
- **Dunnock**
- **Greenfinch**
- **Chaffinch**
- **House Sparrow**

WREN
TROGLODYTES
TROGLODYTES

SONG THRUSH
TURDUS PHILOMELOS

In more suburban areas, with larger gardens, more trees, and more space generally, you might be able to add:

- **House Martin**
- **Goldcrest**
- **Coal Tit**
- **Long-tailed Tit**
- **Goldfinch**
- **Song Thrush**
- **Jay**
- **Mistle Thrush**
- **Pied Wagtail**
- **Sparrowhawk**
- **Lesser Black-backed Gull**
- **Rose-ringed Parakeet (mainly SE England)**
- **Redwing**

If large trees and more extensive bushy habitat are present, additional birds might include:

- **Great Spotted Woodpecker**
- **Green Woodpecker**
- **Jackdaw**
- **Nuthatch**
- **Blackcap**
- **Chiffchaff**
- **Siskin**
- **Bullfinch**
- **Tawny Owl**
- **Spotted Flycatcher**
- **Brambling**

It is quite easy to get to grips with the birds that are likely to occur in your garden. Once you are familiar with the regular visitors, you can start looking out for the more unusual species. Before you know it, you are 'garden-listing'! You can be as lazy as you like in terms of how you attract birds, or you can be quite target-specific, finding out which birds occur in the local area and then setting about encouraging them to visit your own garden.

Habitat Creation and Management

A wildlife-friendly garden does not necessarily mean you have to give it over completely to natural growth and let it become overgrown. By definition, a garden is an area that is managed, a place where nature is shaped and controlled by the gardener. It should also be aesthetic and pleasing to the eye, your very own creative design. Although a garden left completely to nature would make good habitat, you could not really call it a garden.

Man and nature can live happily side by side in a garden, something that wildlife has less chance of doing in the arable countryside these days. Gardens are an increasingly important habitat for bird species, as modern agricultural techniques mean that many species in arable areas have undergone drastic declines in population over the

WAXWING
BOMBYCILLA GARRULUS

last few decades. Song Thrushes, for example, are now more numerous in garden habitats than in the wider countryside.

If you want to plant trees and shrubs to attract birds and other life, ideally you should select native species. This is not obligatory, however, and attractive non-native garden plants can still be useful if they are good nectar-bearers or carry fruit that is useful to native wildlife. Non-native shrubs that bear fruit at the end of the year can certainly draw in birds, such as Redwings and other thrushes, plus the 'holy grail' of garden visitors, the Waxwing. Species of *Cotoneaster* and *Pyracantha* are good, as are ornamental *Sorbus* trees, among others.

Native tree species can be bought very cheaply in bare root form towards the end of the year. When planting trees, it is important to remember that some can get rather big, rather quickly, and may alter the whole feel of your garden by creating large amounts of shade.

This should not stop you experimenting with different trees, however, and you can always cut them back to suit.

There is a wide choice of native shrubs and trees that you may wish to consider:

Alder *Alnus glutinosa*. A fast grower, and in my tiny garden there is a specimen that is already seven metres high just five years after planting! This is a tall and leafy tree, with attractive black cones. I was very excited recently to find my first garden Siskins feeding on these cones, a species I had in mind when I first planted the tree.

Poplars *Populus* sp. Less attractive to birds than the Alder, but worth considering if you want tall growth quickly.

Birch *Betula pubescens* or ***Betula pendula*.** Good trees for birds, supporting many species of insects and also having the green catkins on which Goldfinches like to feed.

Goat Willow *Salix caprea*. Another fast grower, and also supporting many insects. Looks very attractive in the late winter with its yellow catkins, but is a rampant grower and often looks rather messy. Can be a devil to get rid of, as any of its rootlets can sprout into growth.

Hawthorn *Crategus monogyna* and **Blackthorn *Prunus spinosa*** are both ideal hedging plants for the wildlife garden, with attractive blossom in spring and fruits in autumn. They can withstand a lot of cutting and clipping, and will grow into dense hedges offering optimum cover for nesting and roosting birds.

Other attractive and useful native trees are Spindle *Euonymus europaeus*, Guelder Rose *Viburnum opulus*, Wayfaring Tree *V. lantana*, Elder *Sambucus nigra*, Field Maple *Acer campestre*, Hazel *Corylus avellana*, Beech *Fagus sylvatica*, Rowan *Sorbus aucuparia* and other *Sorbus* species. Oak trees *Quercus robur* and *Q. petraea* are very important trees for insects and other life, and host a huge array of caterpillars. If you have one in your garden already, then you are indeed fortunate. They are very slow growing, however, and it would take a long time to see any benefits from the planting of a sapling. Likewise, domestic Apples *Malus domestica* and Crab Apples *M. sylvestris* support much wildlife, but again, they take their time. All these natives are good for insects, which in turn means better habitat for birds, but there are many other flowering plants, both native and non-native, that are useful for attracting a great number of invertebrates. A comprehensive list is beyond the scope of this book, but popular plants favoured by butterflies and other insects include species of Lavender, Hebe, Aubretia and Scabious, as well as Red Valerian *Centranthus ruber*. If it is butterflies that you want to attract, then a Buddleia *Buddleja* sp. is a must. Originally from Asia, these flowering shrubs carry distinctive purple, white or yellow blooms in the summer months, and are much loved by butterflies and bees. They are easy growers and need no attention, but are very vigorous and can become very large, with savage cutting-back only encouraging them

to sprout even more branches! Brambles are very bird-friendly, offering secure nesting sites, flowers that are popular with insects, and fruits that are eaten by a wide range of birds. They may not suit the tidy gardener though, as they quickly become rampant.

It is also worth planting plant species with blooms and seeds that are attractive to birds. Teasel and thistles are a good example. It is very important not to use toxic chemicals and insecticides in your garden, or you will be killing off the very animals that birds like to eat. Various poisons, such as slug pellets, are to be avoided because they may be eaten by ground-feeding birds such as Thrushes and Blackbirds, with fatal consequences.

Ponds

The simplest and most effective thing you can do to increase the diversity of wildlife in your garden is to install a pond. Even the smallest pond will attract invertebrates, amphibians and in turn birds, who

KINGFISHER
ALCEDO ATTHIS

HOUSE MARTIN
DELICHON URBICA

will use it to drink and bathe. If you have just moved into a new home, or have yet to organize the garden space, then you may want to consider putting in a pond first, before you arrange the other features of the garden. Think carefully before you begin as, once in place, ponds are hard to move!

Ponds can be made quite easily, with the main work involved being the digging of the hole. Pre-formed pond liners available in garden centres may be useful, but if you make your own hole then you have more control over the shape, design and depth. Ideally, a pond should have variable depths and at least one sloping edge, so that birds and animals can use the shallower slopes to bathe or to climb in and out. Steep edges are no good for frogs and newts, which then need some kind of ramp in order to get in or out of the water. You will need some Butyl liner, which can be bought off the roll in many garden centres, and once you know how much space you can dedicate to your pond, you will need to calculate the amount of liner required. To do this, you need to work on (length + (deepest depth x2)) x (width + (depth x2)), and add 30–45cm to each figure for the overlap, which is essential for

anchorage. Do not forget to make sure that there is enough liner to overlap the ground level edges. Any unsightly exposed liner can be covered by a roll of fresh turf. Old bits of carpet laid on the soil are useful in providing a barrier between any sharp stones and the liner. The depth of the pond is also quite important. You should make sure that it is at least 60cm in its deepest part, to prevent total freezing in winter.

If the pond is filled with tap water, it should be left for a couple of weeks before adding plants. The best way to fill a pond is with rainwater, and it can be collected via a rain diverter (available in garden centres), attached to a downpipe on the house. This can generate huge amounts of water, and it may be best to route it into a large water butt which can then overflow into the pond; the stored water can be used to top up the pond during dry spells.

A pond will take some time to mature, but you can help it along by adding plants. Make sure you only introduce native pond plants, best sourced from other pond-owning friends, a good garden centre or a pond specialist. If you think you want fish in your pond, then it is a straight choice between fish and other wildlife, such as frogs and newts, as the fish will eat all the tadpoles and other aquatic life. A few logs leading into the water at an angle will enable small creatures to crawl in and out, and it is best not to site the pond under a tree, as in autumn leaves will fall into it, clogging it up and affecting the nutrient balance of the water.

If you are hoping to attract frogs and newts, be sure to create a large brush pile or two nearby, in which they can hibernate. This is easy to make: simply heap up garden waste and cut branches (or logs, if you have any) into a rough pile and leave it undisturbed.

Amphibians will usually find a pond themselves, but you can always kickstart things by adding frogspawn if you know another pond owner that has some. Do not take it from wild ponds. A few rocks and boulders placed in the shallows will provide perches for birds coming to bathe or drink, and hey presto, your pond is alive! Of course, you should also consider whether you want make this

GREEN WOODPECKER JUVENILE
PICUS VIRIDIS

wonderful new feature visible from your vantage point in the house.

Lawns

A garden that is overly manicured, with a tightly cropped lawn and flowerbeds free of any native plants (commonly referred to as weeds!), will not enhance your opportunities for watching birds. You will see some birds, but they are more often just passing through than truly resident. By choosing native plants and trees for your garden, you can quickly convert it into a place in which wildlife wants to forage, enhancing the local populations of invertebrates, which in turn will bring in the birds. The same applies to lawns. There is little attraction for birds in a very short-cropped and tidy lawn, but by letting the grass grow a little, many more invertebrates will be able to use it, and so, in turn, will the birds. The next stage is to leave a few sections to grow even longer, encouraging invertebrates such as beetles and grasshoppers, but how much you are able to indulge yourself with regard to lawns really depends on how you use your garden and how much space you have. Creating a wildflower meadow is one option that may appeal to you if you are seeking to create a really wildlife-friendly garden. Wildflower seed mixes are commercially available, and the native flora will attract many insects, which in turn will benefit the birds.

The structure of your garden will also play a part in terms of the birds you will be able to attract. The tall growth of trees and shrubs may stand out as an island of greenery if surrounding gardens and spaces are without, and so will attract birds into the safe perches and potential breeding sites. Depending on the size of the garden, you may want to restrict the amount of growth in order to see more clearly what is going on, either from your vantage point within the house or as you sit out on a warm summer's afternoon. Wider open spaces may bring in larger birds, or allow ground-feeding species to feed undisturbed; for this they need a clear view all around, to allow them early warning of marauding predators, alongside proximity to cover to which they can retreat when danger looms.

Pests and Predators

It should be said first of all that one person's pest might be another person's cuddly countryside creature! However, the fact remains that birds are subject to a range of predators, natural and otherwise, and in the garden environment these can be artificially concentrated, sometimes reaching pest proportions and having a serious impact on bird populations and behaviour.

Grey Squirrels are a major pest in Britain, robbing birds' nests of eggs and young, and are thought to be responsible for the recent declines in species such as Spotted Flycatcher. They also cause damage to bird feeders by gnawing through plastic. An effective remedy is to buy squirrel-proof feeders to discourage them from visiting your garden.

Rats are also a nuisance, and will rob nests of eggs and young. They are attracted to bird seed spillage and to food scraps thrown on the ground, so beware of allowing your feeding stations to become too messy. Always wear gloves when handling your bird feeders, as rats can be vectors for disease.

Cats are incredibly damaging to wildlife. They are almost impossible to keep out of a garden, and frequently reach pest proportions in many suburban areas. It is estimated that cats kill 15 Robins for every one taken by a natural predator such as a Sparrowhawk. This is an awkward subject, on which emotions can run high. Cat-owners sometimes struggle to understand the impact that their pets are having on local bird populations, but at the same time one must acknowledge the great pleasure cats can give to their owners. Indeed, many bird-lovers are also cat-owners. Although the bottom line remains that cats will kill birds, there are various ways in which the level of destruction can be reduced.

SPOTTED FLYCATCHER JUVENILE
MUSCICAPA STRIATA

BLACKBIRD
TURDUS MERULA

On the basis that prevention is usually better than cure, keeping cats out of the garden in the first place is the best option, however difficult to achieve! One measure you can introduce, to try and frustrate their ingress, is to block corners and any gaps in the garden perimeter with branches cut from brambles and other spiky plants, and perhaps shield areas where birds come to feed with spiky palisades to hamper the progress of intruders. Hedging with Hawthorn or other densely growing shrubs can help, or you can attach obstacles to the tops of fences where cats jump over, such as expanding trellis strips laid lengthways. There are also some electronic repellent devices available, whereby a unit emits a signal that is disliked by cats. If elaborate palisades and access points are so arranged that the only way in for a cat is guarded by one of these, then they may be effective. However, there is evidence that cats will learn to adapt their routes around these devices, rather than be scared away completely.

Chasing away cats on foot can bring short-term success, but is rather labour-intensive and it can be difficult to maintain 24-hour coverage! The success of physical deterrents largely depends on hitting the target, and it should always be borne in mind that it is illegal to knowingly cause suffering to a cat. However, a water pistol will usually yield results, without harming the animal, and if used regularly, the cat may eventually react just to the sound of a window or door opening which usually precedes the attack, so that before long your garden could be largely free of cats during daylight hours. Failing that, get yourself a dog!

If cat presence in a garden is terminated suddenly, it is remarkable how quickly small birds will reappear. In cases where cats cannot be totally excluded from a garden, it is worth asking their owners to attach a small bell to their pet's collar. The noise of the bell, as the cat rushes forward towards its intended prey, gives birds a critical split second warning, which is often time enough for them to take flight. Evidence suggests that cats with bells on their collars catch up to 40 per cent fewer birds than those without.

Nest Boxes and Nesting

Nest boxes are a great way to study the lives, ecology and behaviour of birds in the garden, and over sixty different species have been recorded using them. Although next boxes vary considerably in terms of the precise arrangements required to attract particular species, they are usually simple wooden structures that can be homemade or bought from an ever-increasing array of retailers.

One issue that must be considered when thinking of erecting a nest box is how busy the garden is. During the breeding season birds are strongly territorial, and if a box is sited too near to feeding stations, then it is unlikely to be occupied – the stress of having to chase away so many visitors would be too much! A quiet place, at least five metres from any feeding point, would be satisfactory. It is also important to locate a nest box where it is secure from predators such as cats, rats and squirrels; open boxes definitely require a discreet and hidden location, as they are also at risk of predation by corvids. As Great Spotted Woodpeckers will attack nest boxes to take small chicks, hole-entrance boxes can be protected by fixing a metal plate with a hole of the same dimensions over the front of the box, preventing woodpeckers from enlarging the hole and reaching the young inside.

The classic bird nest box is a wooden structure with a sloping roof, and a round hole cut in the upper front plate. The diameter of the entrance hole will determine possible occupants:

25mm: **Blue Tit, Coal Tit**
28mm: **Great Tit, Tree Sparrow, House Sparrow**
32mm: **House Sparrow, Nuthatch, Pied Flycatcher**
45mm: **Starling**
50mm: **Green, Greater and Lesser Spotted Woodpeckers**
150mm: **Jackdaw, Stock Dove**

Robins, Wrens, Pied Wagtails and Spotted Flycatchers prefer a box with half the front panel open. Among the larger birds that will use nest boxes, Kestrels favour a square, open-fronted box, 150mm deep by 50mm wide, with an overhanging roof. Tawny and Barn Owls will use a box that is open on one side, with a base of 200mm square and sides 750mm high. They also like the box to be mounted under the shelter of eaves or a large branch, and angled at 45 degrees to the wall or branch. A special artificial nest can encourage House Martins and Swallows. Swifts will also use nest boxes designed specifically for them, but have to be lured in with sound recordings before they will inspect them. Further information about the many different types of nest box is available from the websites of bird protection societies such as the RSPB or BTO in the UK and increasingly from specialist bird feed suppliers.

It is important for a bird box to have a sloping and overlapping roof to divert excess rain, and drainage holes drilled through the floor panel to prevent waterlogging. For most species the box should be placed as high as possible on a wall or tree, well out of harm's way, but for smaller open-front box nesters, such as Robin and Wren, it needs to be located fairly low down (20–120cm off the ground) and partly or wholly hidden from general view. The box needs to open easily for cleaning at the end of each breeding season, an essential procedure for which a hinged roof should suffice. Be sure to remove any old nesting material and use boiling water to kill any remaining parasites and bugs, allowing the box to dry out thoroughly afterwards. Some nest boxes for small birds often have a removable upper half to the front plate, so you can choose or alternate between having a hole-entrance box or an open-fronted box. Taking care to ensure that they are securely fixed, boxes should always be placed on north- or east-facing walls or trees, thereby avoiding the hottest sun (from the south) and wet prevailing winds (largely from the west). Beware of cheaper boxes with thin walls – thicker walls provide better insulation against temperature extremes and rainfall.

Nest boxes should be erected no later than February, as any later than this and the birds may have already selected a nesting place. Boxes should also be left in place during the winter, as birds may use them as roosting places. Of course, not all the nest boxes in a garden will be used every year, and sometimes not by the species for which they are intended! I erected a 'House Sparrow terrace', a large box with three separate units, each with their own hole, as there are many House Sparrows in my area. I have never seen a House Sparrow even look at the box, but it is used successfully by Blue Tits and Great Tits in alternate years!

Providing nest material is also an option if you want to give birds further help. Hair, wool, feathers from old pillows, cotton and straw are all useful items, and these can either be scattered about or made available via a tidy, dedicated nest-material point, such as a piece of wire mesh attached to a tree trunk. If you have a large enough garden pond with muddy edges, House Martins can collect

PIED FLYCATCHER
FICEDULA HYPOLEUCA

their building materials here, and are more likely to nest on your house than if they have to find a mud source elsewhere.

Care should be taken during the breeding season not to disturb nest boxes or open the lids to look in and see if there are eggs or young. If you really want to see what is going on inside, it is possible to buy a unit with a small camera similar to a webcam, allowing the nest to be monitored from your computer or TV. These can be purchased from the websites of bird protection societies such as the RSPB in the UK.

Feeding Garden Birds

Providing food for birds in your garden is a sure way of encouraging them to visit. There are two ways in which you can do this. One is to ensure that there is a range of natural food available, through the planting of the appropriate species of tree and shrub to provide invertebrate food, seeds and berries (see pages 12–13). The other way is to provide artificial foodstuffs. Although this is perhaps more crucial in the winter months, it has been shown that feeding throughout the year is important. In the breeding season, live foods are popular with many birds and bulky foods are to be avoided as they can choke nestlings. Fatty offerings are taken at all times of year, but especially in winter. Seeds can be offered throughout the year.

Garden feeding has expanded hugely in recent years, with all kinds of bird-focused food and feeders now available in the retail market, with even some of the big supermarkets now offering food and feeders at knock-down prices. This phenomenon has doubtless been fuelled by the ever-increasing popularity of garden birding. Years ago, people would have put food out for the birds in order to bring them closer to their final destination of the cooking pot! More recently, many of us began by throwing bread on to the lawn for the birds or by putting out peanuts in the red mesh bags that became popular in the 1970s. These days, lucrative businesses are thriving thanks to the demand in food for garden birds, and today's choice of products is greater than ever.

There are two things to consider when feeding the birds in your garden. The first is where to locate the feeders within your garden, and the second is which food you are going to provide, with the kind of feeder used dependent on this choice. The location of feeders is important, as you will want to place them in a good position for the birds you are trying to attract, considering the potential predators that may be attracted to a busy feeding station as well as your own ability to watch the birds whilst they feed. The simplest method of feeding birds is from a bird table. While there are many types of elaborate shop-bought tables, they are actually very simple to make yourself. All you need is a tray, with holes in it for drainage, erected on a pole. Protection from the elements is another issue, and some commercially available bird tables have a roof, which will keep the food dry, and side edges, which help prevent food from blowing away. The height of the table is entirely up to you, although it must be positioned in a place that cats cannot easily reach or sneak up on. Lower tables, that sit just off the ground or up to 50cm high, will attract ground-feeding birds such as Blackbirds, Song Thrushes and Robins, while higher tables better suit small birds such as Tits and Finches. Tables

REDWING
TURDUS ILIACUS

should also be located reasonably close to cover, so that birds can retreat to safety at the first sign of danger. This applies particularly in areas where Sparrowhawks are present, as these are a constant hazard for small birds at feeding stations.

Other threats include squirrels and rats, which are attracted to the food itself. Squirrels can be a major nuisance, as they come and steal the food that is intended for the birds and they can badly damage plastic feeders by gnawing through the fittings in order to reach the contents. It is possible to buy squirrel-proof feeders that have a baffle or cage-like structure that prevents them from doing this. Rats may be attracted to food thrown on the ground, but they are usually nocturnal and so less likely to be seen. The occurrence of both these pests is highly detrimental to nesting birds, so they should always be discouraged.

One of the main reasons for feeding birds is so you can watch them come to your garden. It is therefore important to locate feeders where you have a clear view of the action. Once you have decided on the location of your feeders, then you have to decide what feed you are going to provide.

Peanuts are perhaps the commonest available bird food and constitute a valuable energy source. Most birds will eat peanuts, although not always in their whole form. The peanut granules that are sometimes mixed in with seed are generally popular, and it is also possible to buy them as a pure feed from specialist suppliers. It is important to offer whole peanuts in a mesh feeder, because if small birds offer whole peanuts to their offspring then the youngsters may choke. Peanut feeders are typically made of an open metal mesh, with holes small enough to keep the nuts in but adequately large for the birds to access them. They come in fairly standard shapes, with the cheapest ones being made of plastic and the more expensive examples in metal, the latter being easier to clean. Like most things in life, with bird feeders you get what you pay for, but the cheaper feeders are still useful if you have not yet settled on exactly which feeders are best for your garden. The same goes for the feed itself. Cheaper peanuts may be infected with aflatoxins, which are poisonous to birds, so it is best to buy peanuts from a reputable source that specifies that the peanuts are aflatoxin-free.

Seed mixes are popular with even more birds than are attracted to peanuts. Many different species will come to seed feeders, and there is a wide variety of seed on sale. Seed feeders are usually plastic tubes with openings through which the seed can be accessed, ideally with a small perch for the visitors to sit on. Nyger seed feeders are similar in form but with smaller holes.

The most energy-rich seeds are generally the priciest, and feeding birds can become expensive, especially if you have a resident gang of 30 House Sparrows systematically emptying your feeders on a daily basis! You may want to experiment with different kinds of seed, in which case it makes sense to start with one of the widely available cheap mixes. Many different bird species will be attracted by these, but such mixes are often bulked up by types of seed that do not appeal to certain species and particularly by wheat, which is especially loved by pigeons and doves. You may therefore choose to site seed feeders in a place where Woodpigeons cannot access them, because otherwise they may strip your feeders bare in a very short time!

Using mixed seed in hanging feeders may produce a lot of waste, but the exact cost-versus-waste ratio is difficult to assess. House Sparrows in particular are

BLACKCAP
SYLVIA ATRICAPILLA

quite fussy, and will sit at a feeder throwing aside all the unwanted seed, which ends up on the ground. In my garden, the Collared Doves and House Sparrows seem to have a symbiotic relationship. While the sparrows swarm around the feeders, the doves (which thrive on the cheap mixed seed) come in and clean up the seed that falls below. The sparrows are searching particularly for the black sunflower seed that is mixed in with the other seed. Black sunflower seeds are very attractive to sparrows and finches, and can be bought on their own, although they are more expensive. One option is to buy a bag of black sunflower seeds and a bag of mixed seed, and then mix them together to create a richer seed mix. More costly, but probably the most attractive feed to the widest selection of birds, are sunflower hearts. In this case the shell has been removed, leaving just the energy-rich nugget at the centre.

If you want to attract Goldfinches, then it is worth purchasing a nyger seed feeder. Nyger seed is very small and thin, rather like a thistle seed, and has to be hung in a particular kind of feeder with very narrow holes to prevent the seed falling out. Goldfinches and Siskins adore this seed, and are able to access it through the small holes, thanks to their narrow pointed bills. Once they have located a source of nyger seed, they will be there religiously every day! Other species, such as Greenfinch and House Sparrow, will also visit nyger seed feeders occasionally.

Other seeds that are attractive to birds and can be bought from specialist suppliers are millet, oats, rapeseed, hemp, safflower, quinoa, pumpkin, buckwheat, rice, millet, poppy seed, canary seed, Sorghum, rye, wheat, maize, barley and linseed. Nuts and pulses that can be fed to birds include chick peas, lentils, mung beans and peas. Coconut is also a very popular food, and half a coconut hanging from a branch or bird table makes an ideal bird feeder. Fat balls are very popular with certain species, and are widely available in various sizes. They can be hung by their mesh bag or, better still, inserted into a fat ball feeder, a simple metal mesh with very large holes that are still small enough to keep the fat ball inside. Smaller species such as tits find them attractive, as do sparrows and Starlings. Indeed, a group of Starlings can quickly devour a fat ball in a very short time. Also available commercially are a wide variety of suet and peanut cakes, which can also be very popular with your garden visitors. Of course, it is possible to make 'bird cakes' at home out of unwanted fat with a few seeds mixed in. These are invaluable in cold weather, when the birds really need the extra energy.

Food scraps can be offered, either on a bird table or wedged into a fat ball feeder. Fat cut from meat, such as bacon rind, should be chopped smaller to make it more digestible for smaller birds. Fruit is also good, with windfall apples being particularly attractive to Blackbirds and thrushes. Raisins and currants are also a good thrush food, but beware if you have a dog, as these fruits can cause canine renal problems. Bread still seems to have a wide appeal, and throwing bread into an open area can often attract gulls, as well as the gangs of Starlings that seem to dominate such offerings.

Live food such as mealworms can be important (especially for Robins) and is the best kind of food to put out during the breeding season, when even seed-eating birds will be feeding their young on caterpillars and similar invertebrates. Birds nesting in gardens often have smaller broods and lower breeding success than their relatives in more optimal habitat, and this may be due to the reduced availability of

insect food in a garden situation. By feeding live food you can go part of the way to correct that balance. Mealworms should be offered in a small tray or bowl with raised sides so that they do not wriggle out, and they are also available in dead or dried form.

It is important not to forget water for birds. A raised birdbath is ideal, and, as with bird feeders, you must ensure that it is located in a safe place, where cats cannot get to it. Birds will often want to drink and bathe, particularly in hot weather. Ponds are ideal for this purpose (see pages 13–14).

List of main garden species and preferred foods

Species	Preferred foods
Great Spotted Woodpecker	Live food, peanuts, cake mixes, sunflower seeds, seed mixes
Green Woodpecker	Live food
Collared Dove	Seed mixes
Woodpigeon	Seed mixes
Robin	Live food, peanut granules
Dunnock	Peanut granules, small seeds in mixes
Wren	Live food, peanut granules
Blackbird	Live food, peanut granules, fruit
Song Thrush	Live food, peanut granules, fruit
Blue Tit	Cake mixes, seed mixes, peanuts, sunflower seeds
Great Tit	Cake mixes, seed mixes, peanuts, sunflower seeds
Coal Tit	Cake mixes, seed mixes, peanuts, sunflower seeds
Long-tailed Tit	Cake mixes, sunflower seeds, peanuts, peanut granules
Starling	Almost anything
Pied Wagtail	Live food
Nuthatch	Cake mixes, peanuts, sunflower seeds
Blackcap	Live food, peanut granules, fruit
Goldfinch	Seed mixes, peanuts, sunflower seeds, nyger seed
Siskin	Seed mixes, peanuts, sunflower seeds, nyger seed
Bullfinch	Seed mixes, sunflower seeds
Brambling	Live food, small seeds in mixes
Greenfinch	Seed mixes, sunflower seeds, nyger seed
Chaffinch	Seed mixes, peanut granules
House Sparrow	Live food, seed mixes, sunflower seeds

Garden Bird Calendar

This table gives you a general idea of what birds you are likely to see, and when, in your garden. While some species are found in Britain and Northern Europe all year round, others are only present during either the winter or summer. However, you may see species of bird which, while resident in the region throughout the year, only appear in your garden during certain months, such as gulls in winter. These visiting patterns are usually dictated by geography and topography, but there are no hard and fast rules in the complex world of birds.

Status:	R = resident	SV = Summer visitor	WV = Winter visitor
	MV = migrant visitor	WSC = scarce winter visitor	SSC = scarce summer visitor
	● = possible garden visitor	■ = likely garden visitor	

Page	Birds	Status	Jan	Feb	Mar	Apr	May	Jun	Jul	Aug	Sep	Oct	Nov	Dec
26	Mallard	R	●	●	●	●	●	●	●	●	●	●	●	●
28	Red-legged Partridge	R	●	●	●	●	●	●	●	●	●	●	●	●
30	Pheasant	R	●	●	●	●	●	●	●	●	●	●	●	●
32	Grey Heron	R	●	●	●	●	●	●	●	●	●	●	●	●
34	Red Kite	R	●	●	●	●	●	●	●	●	●	●	●	●
36	Sparrowhawk	R	■	■	■	■	■	■	■	■	■	■	■	■
38	Buzzard	R	●	●	●	●	●	●	●	●	●	●	●	●
40	Kestrel	R	●	●	●	●	●	●	●	●	●	●	●	●
42	Hobby	SV/SSC					●	●	●	●	●			
44	Moorhen	R	●	●	●	●	●	●	●	●	●	●	●	●
46	Oystercatcher	R/MV/WSC	●	●	●	●	●	●	●	●	●	●	●	●
48	Lapwing	R/MV/WSC	●	●	●	●	●	●	●	●	●	●	●	●
50	Woodcock	R/MV/WSC	●	●	●	●	●	●	●	●	●	●	●	●
52	Black-headed Gull	R	■	■	■	■	●	●	●	●	■	■	■	■
54	Common Gull	R/WV	■	■	■	■				■	■	■	■	■
56	Lesser Black-backed Gull	R	■	■	■	■	●	●	●	■	■	■	■	■
58	Herring Gull	R/MV	●	●	●	●	●	●	●	●	●	●	●	●
60	Feral Pigeon	R	●	●	●	●	●	●	●	●	●	●	●	●
62	Stock Dove	R	●	●	●	●	●	●	●	●	●	●	●	●
64	Woodpigeon	R	■	■	■	■	■	■	■	■	■	■	■	■
66	Collared Dove	R	■	■	■	■	■	■	■	■	■	■	■	■
68	Turtle Dove	SV/MV					●	●	●	●	●			
70	Rose-ringed Parakeet	R	●	●	●	●	●	●	●	●	●	●	●	●
72	Cuckoo	SV				●	●	●	●					
74	Barn Owl	R	●	●	●	●	●	●	●	●	●	●	●	●
76	Little Owl	R	●	●	●	●	●	●	●	●	●	●	●	●
78	Tawny Owl	R	●	●	●	●	●	●	●	●	●	●	●	●
80	Swift	SV					■	■	■	■				
82	Kingfisher	R/MV/WSC	●	●	●	●	●	●	●	●	●	●	●	●
84	Green Woodpecker	R	■	■	■	■	■	■	■	■	■	■	■	■
86	Great Spotted Woodpecker	R	■	■	■	■	■	■	■	■	■	■	■	■
88	Lesser Spotted Woodpecker	R	●	●	●	●	●	●	●	●	●	●	●	●
90	Skylark	R/MV	●	●	●	●	●	●	●	●	●	●	●	●
92	Swallow	SV				●	●	●	●	●	●			
94	House Martin	SV					■	■	■	■	■			
96	Meadow Pipit	R/MV/WSC	●	●	●	●	●	●	●	●	●	●	●	●
98	Grey Wagtail	R/WV	●	●	●	●	●	●	●	●	●	●	●	●

Page	Birds	Status	Jan	Feb	Mar	Apr	May	Jun	Jul	Aug	Sep	Oct	Nov	Dec
100	Pied/White Wagtail	R	■	■	■	■	■	■	■	■	■	■	■	■
102	Waxwing	WSC	●	●	●							●	●	●
104	Wren	R	■	■	■	■	■	■	■	■	■	■	■	■
106	Dunnock	R	■	■	■	■	■	■	■	■	■	■	■	■
108	Robin	R	■	■	■	■	■	■	■	■	■	■	■	■
110	Blackbird	R	■	■	■	■	■	■	■	■	■	■	■	■
112	Fieldfare	WV/MV	■	■	■	●						●	■	■
114	Song Thrush	R	■	■	■	■	■	■	■	■	■	■	■	■
116	Redwing	WV/MV	■	■	■	●						●	■	■
118	Mistle Thrush	R	■	■	■	■	■	■	■	■	■	■	■	■
120	Blackcap	SV/WSC	●	●	●	■	■	■	■	■	■	●	●	●
122	Garden Warbler	SV/MV				●	●	●	●	●	●			
124	Lesser Whitethroat	SV/MV				●	●	●	●	●	●			
126	Common Whitethroat	SV/MV				●	●	●	●	●	●			
128	Chiffchaff	SV/WSC	●	●	■	■	■	■	■	■	■	●	●	●
130	Willow Warbler	SV				●	●	●	●	●	●			
132	Goldcrest	R/MV	■	■	■	■	■	■	■	■	■	■	■	■
134	Spotted Flycatcher	SV/MV					●	●	●	●	●			
136	Pied Flycatcher	SV/MV				●	●	●	●	●	●			
138	Long-tailed Tit	R	■	■	■	■	■	■	■	■	■	■	■	■
140	Blue Tit	R	■	■	■	■	■	■	■	■	■	■	■	■
142	Great Tit	R	■	■	■	■	■	■	■	■	■	■	■	■
144	Coal Tit	R	■	■	■	■	■	■	■	■	■	■	■	■
146	Willow Tit	R/WSC	●	●	●	●	●	●	●	●	●	●	●	●
148	Marsh Tit	R/WSC	●	●	●	●	●	●	●	●	●	●	●	●
150	Nuthatch	R	■	■	●	●	●	●	●	●	●	●	●	●
152	Treecreeper	R	●	●	●	●	●	●	●	●	●	●	●	●
154	Jay	R	■	■	●	■	■	■	■	■	■	■	■	■
156	Magpie	R	■	■	■	■	■	■	■	■	■	■	■	■
158	Jackdaw	R	■	■	■	■	■	■	■	■	■	■	■	■
160	Rook	R	●	●	●	●	●	●	●	●	●	●	●	●
162	Carrion Crow/Hooded Crow	R	■	■	■	■	■	■	■	■	■	■	■	■
164	Starling	R	●	●	●	●	●	●	●	●	●	●	●	●
166	House Sparrow	R	●	●	●	●	●	●	●	●	●	●	●	●
168	Tree Sparrow	R	●	●	●	●	●	●	●	●	●	●	●	●
170	Chaffinch	R	■	■	■	■	■	■	■	■	■	■	■	■
172	Brambling	WV	●	●	●	●								
174	Greenfinch	R	■	■	■	■	■	■	■	■	■	■	■	■
176	Goldfinch	R	■	■	■	■	■	■	■	■	■	■	■	■
178	Siskin	R/WV	■	■	■	●	●	●	●	●	●	■	■	■
180	Linnet	R/WV	●	●	●	●	●	●	●	●	●	●	●	●
182	Lesser Redpoll	R/WV	●	●	●	●	●	●	●	●	●	●	●	●
184	Common Crossbill	R/MV	●	●	●	●	●	●	●	●	●	●	●	●
186	Bullfinch	R	●	●	●	●	●	●	●	●	●	●	●	●
188	Hawfinch	R/WSC	●	●	●	●	●	●	●	●	●	●	●	●
190	Yellowhammer	R/WSC	●	●	●	●	●	●	●	●	●	●	●	●
192	Reed Bunting	R/WSC	●	●	●	●	●	●	●	●	●	●	●	●

Mallard
Anas platyrhynchos

Length: 50–65cm
Wingspan: 81–98cm

MALE

A familiar bird which, like most other duck species, shows a marked plumage difference between the sexes. The male is a distinctive and fairly robust bird, with a long neck, dirty-yellow bill, glossy bottle-green head, white neck ring, purple-brown breast and ash-grey belly sides and upperparts. During the months of July to October the male moults into eclipse plumage, which when complete is similar to the female's coloration but darker and more uniform. The wing has a bold speculum of blue or purple, which changes colour depending on the light and is bordered by black and white lines, a constant feature in both sexes and all plumages. The demure female is brown, streaked and spotted overall with black, with a darker crown and eye-stripe. The bill is dull orange- or olive-coloured, with a dark culmen and tip. The downy chicks are marbled yellowish and dark brown, graduating into a brown juvenile plumage similar to that of the female.

MALE

FEMALE

Common and widespread, the Mallard is extremely tolerant of humans and very adaptable. Indeed, in many localities it is positively tame, with feral populations occupying urban and ornamental lakes where truly wild birds would not typically be seen. In Britain, resident populations are supplemented in winter by migrants arriving from Iceland and other parts of northern and north-western Europe. It is found in an amazingly wide range of wetland habitats, including shallow coasts, rivers, lakes, marshes, ditches and man-made water bodies such as reservoirs, parks, ponds, and it will use arable fields for grazing. It always favours shallow water, and can often be seen up-ending as it feeds on underwater vegetation. During courtship the males will chase females in wide-ranging flights, which often feature several males in pursuit, and at this time birds can be seen readily from gardens, even when located some distance from water. Breeding commences in March, with typically 10–12 eggs being laid (although the number can vary from 7–16) and incubation carried out solely by the female, for 28–29 days. The nest is lined with vegetable matter and down, and is typically on the ground in a sheltered place with fairly thick cover, such as bushes or tall vegetation. Suitable niches in trees or other elevated places are used on occasion. The nest is usually within reach of fresh water, and wild and undisturbed gardens are used if these conditions are met. The young will be led to water by the mother soon after hatching, and are aquatically adept from a very young age. The chicks are fully fledged after 7–8 weeks; meanwhile, the adult males form bachelor parties, moulting into their eclipse plumage in the summer months. Pairing occurs in autumn.

The calls of the male and female differ somewhat. The male gives a soft nasal "rrheerrb" or "queep", and when in group he often accompanies this with a low quacking "rhu-rhu-rhu-rhu…". The female gives the classic "quack-quack" call. This is typically in a series of 2–10 notes, with the stress on the first two quacks and then tailing off, such as "Qwah Qwah Qwa qwa wha wha wha wha…". It is frequently uttered, often when flushed or when other Mallards are in the air nearby. The female also gives various permutations of these calls, with persistent quacks when advertising, or low chuntering quacks when with young, which themselves give a high-pitched "peepee" contact call.

FEMALE WITH CHICKS

Red-legged Partridge
Alectoris rufa

Length: 32–34cm
Wingspan: 47–50cm

A dumpy short-legged gamebird, the Red-legged differs from the Grey Partridge in having a bold black bridle through the eye, curving down across the top of the breast to enclose a white throat. The upper breast is marked with a necklace of black spots stretching down from the black throat-ring. It has a whitish supercilium outlining a grey-and-brown crown, and the bill, eye-ring and of course the legs, are all bright red. The flanks are greyish, boldly marked with vertical bands of black and chestnut and thin whitish lines. The lower breast is grey, the belly is rich ochre, and the upperparts are a dull olive-brown. In flight it shows a rusty tail, a feature shared with the Grey Partridge, although only the Red-legged has a grey rump.

Frequently found in arable habitats, it can use a diverse range of cultivated and open country, preferring lowlands but occurring in mountainous areas up to 2000m in the southern part of its range. It enjoys sunny places, with some barren patches and low vegetation providing open areas with good visibility and access. Small parties are often

seen scuttling across bare fields or running startled along country roadsides. Restricted to western Europe and sedentary throughout its range, the population in Britain was begun with an introduction from France in the eighteenth century. It is now the most commonly encountered partridge in England, and is slowly spreading its population in Scotland and Wales. Established populations are often supplemented with mass releases for shooting, sometimes numbering in the thousands. It is at this time that they are most likely to appear in gardens, perhaps feeding on seed spilt from feeders, and particularly in more rural areas adjoining suitable farmland habitat.

For nesting the male prepares a scrape in low vegetation, which is lined with leaves and grass, and 10–16 eggs are laid at 36-hour intervals. Incredibly, incubation does not commence immediately, and the eggs can sit for some time before incubation begins. In addition to this strange behaviour, the female can lay two clutches in two separate nests soon after one another, and she incubates one while the male incubates the other! After hatching, each adult tends its own personal brood separately. Incubation typically lasts 23–24 days, with the young leaving the nest soon after hatching and being able to fly after two weeks. These family groups stay together until the start of the following breeding season.

Commonly heard in farmland, with their gruff calls emanating from crops and field margins. The main call begins with a few hoarse notes and accelerates into a "gochok-chok-chokhrrr" or "kaku'kaku'kuk'ukhurr", repeated rhythmically. The advertising call of the male is a similar "gochak-chak-chak go-chak go chak-chak", and they can also give a "kot'tach'eh" and "uh'uh'akh'akh'aar". When flushed they can give a sharp, harsh "schtregh-schtrregh", which is also uttered on the ground as a predator-alert call. Various other conversational chuntering calls are given in different social situations.

FEMALE WITH CHICKS

Pheasant
Phasianus colchicus

Length: male 66–89cm (inc. tail of 35–54cm),
female 53–63cm
Wingspan: 70–90cm

The male Pheasant is unmistakable, a big and brightly plumaged bird with a long olive-brown and black-barred tail, a metallic green head with a large red wattle around the eyes, little tufts at the rear of the crown and a copper-coloured body marked with black and pale grey scallops. The female is a uniform buff-brown all over, with darker brown spotting along the flanks and dark feather centres on the mantle, and a slightly shorter tail. Juveniles are similar to the female, although they do not develop a long tail until their first autumn. Introduced into western Europe many centuries ago, many thousands are now bred and released for shooting. The plumage can be highly variable owing to different races having being released, but the common form typically has a white neck-ring. The natural range extends from north Turkey across to China, and there is a large number of different races with varying plumage characteristics.

Commonly encountered in farmland, where it favours crop fields, pastures and rough ground, woodland edges and open woodland, it can also be found in scrub and in reedbeds, indeed anywhere that is a little damp with good ground cover. In their natural range they are shy, and can be found in similar habitats, also extending into the foothills of mountain ranges or into semi-desert regions where water is present.

Breeding takes place between early April and early June, the female laying 7–15 eggs on consecutive days and then doing all the

MALE

incubation, which lasts for 22–27 days. The nest is a hollow scrape sparsely lined with grasses or similar, on the ground and well hidden in dense cover such as tall grass, bushes and overgrown herbage. It will readily nest in a large wild garden if undisturbed, particularly in rural villages or on the edges of urban areas if adjacent to its favoured habitats. It will also visit gardens in these localities to feed on spilt grain or insects and invertebrates. The chicks are usually pale buff, unmarked below and patterned with dark brown above. They leave the nest soon after hatching, and are tended, fed and brooded solely by the female, and able to fly after 12–14 days.

The display or advertising call of the male is a loud and far-carrying "karck-kahk!" or "aarrkh-ukh", often followed immediately by an audible quick whirr of the wings. This is usually delivered with the head pointing upwards, and sometimes from a raised perch. Any loud noise can trigger this call, even something as artificial as the slamming of a car door! Both sexes can be noisy when flushed, making some loud "kh'kh'k!" or "uuk-ukh! uuk-ukh!" calls as they go, and often exploding vertically out of cover when surprised. The female also has a piping whistle, and both sexes can utter a soft and conversational double "uh-urh" in the breeding season. The chicks make a high-pitched peeping contact note.

MALE

FEMALE

Grey Heron
Ardea cinerea

Length: 90–102cm

Wingspan: 175–195cm

One of our most commonly encountered large birds, the Grey Heron is often seen standing motionless at the water's edge, waiting for prey to come within striking range. A long-necked, long-legged bird that is uniform mid-grey on the upperparts when seen at rest, in flight it shows blackish-grey flight feathers with two small,whitish patches on the leading edge, and has a distinctive flight silhouette of wings strongly bowed. The underparts are white with variable amounts of a grey wash on the lower neck, and on the breast it has a chain of black markings forming two vertical lines. The head is primarily white, with a central white crown-stripe and black crown-sides extending into an elongated nape plume in the adult, or with a grey crown in immature

ADULT
SPRING
PLUMAGE

birds. The bill is greenish-yellow, turning pale orange in the breeding season, or intense flame-orange during courtship.

The Grey Heron favours a wide variety of habitats – basically wherever there is water shallow enough for it wade and search for food. Its main prey item is fish, although it will also take frogs, water voles, small birds and various other types of live prey. It frequents either standing or flowing fresh- or saltwater, in rivers, streams, marshes, estuaries, floods, lakes, ponds and reservoirs, and outside the breeding season can occur on beaches, lagoons and inlets. Airborne birds going to and from feeding areas are easily seen from gardens, and birds can turn up actually in gardens if a pond with fish is present, much to the annoyance of the householder if prize specimens are kept there!

A colonial breeder, it typically nests in tall trees with up to 10 nests per tree, although on occasion it will nest singly in low bushes or on the ground in undisturbed places. Urban areas are no barrier to Grey Herons, as the London colonies at Regent's Park and Walthamstow Reservoirs demonstrate. The nest is a platform of twigs, often reused and added to year after year so that it can become a very bulky mass. The male brings the twigs and the female does the building, with breeding commencing in February or early March. Both sexes incubate the three or four eggs for 23–28 days, and the chicks are fed by both parents, remaining in the nest for 50–55 days.

The most familiar call is a loud "frahnk!" or "raahnk!" that is given in flight and often repeated by flying birds every few seconds. A less emphatic version of this call is also repeated when a bird comes in to land. A variety of other calls is given at the breeding colony, such as a sharp yelping "hrow!" or "aaow!", given by the male when advertising for a mate. Various harsh crowing and cooing sounds are uttered at different stages of courtship and nesting, including a throaty "ga'ga'ga'ga", a lower-pitched "wark'wark'wark" and a rasping "aaaagh".

Red Kite
Milvus milvus

Length: 60–66cm
Wingspan: 175–195cm

Along with the Common Buzzard, this is perhaps the only large raptor that is likely to be encountered over inhabited areas. Introductions in various parts of Britain are turning this bird from a rarity, previously restricted to central Wales, into a common sight in some counties, where it is likely to become much more of a regular 'garden' bird. It has a distinctive flight silhouette of long, fairly narrow wings, which in typical foraging flight are held loosely in a slightly bowed fashion, with long glides interspersed with deep, elastic wingbeats. Its tail, markedly forked and auburn-red to buffy brown in colour with black corners, is twisted and tilted like a rudder as the bird slowly circles and hangs in the wind, head facing downwards as its eyes scour the ground below. The body is a rich rufous-orange boldly striated with black, while the head is whitish-grey. The mantle is a black-streaked rufous-brown, and in flight the upperwing shows blackish-brown flight feathers and a paler buffy panel across the wing coverts. The underwing is strikingly patterned with black wingtips and blackish secondaries, a large whitish patch on the inner and middle primaries, rusty underwing coverts and a blackish band along the tips of the coverts forming a prominent bar.

Breeds in deciduous woodlands, and can be found around woods and copses adjacent to open country, in lowlands and hills up to 600m. Usually avoiding dense forest, it can frequently be seen over open country as it forages for carrion, its main source of food, although it will also hunt small

prey. In Britain it has been reintroduced to many former areas of occurrence, and in some counties of the Midlands and south-east England it has become fairly common in recent years. It can be seen foraging over arable fields, along roadsides and wooded edges, and it also regularly visits rubbish tips. While it may be readily seen overhead from gardens in these reintroduction areas, sometimes it can be lured in to take scraps of meat from garden lawns and open areas provided there is enough room for these large birds to fly down, snatch the item and get away again without stopping! Reintroduced birds often have a numbered wing-tag that is visible in flight, although the actual number may be visible only with a close view. Shakespeare mentions this species no fewer than 15 times in his works, evidence that they were a common urban scavenger in London in the late sixteenth and early seventeenth centuries.

The nest is built in a tall tree and is made of sticks and debris, with the old nest of a Buzzard or Raven sometimes being utilized. Both sexes help with construction, with the male bringing twigs for the female to arrange in the nest. Breeding begins in April (or earlier in the south of its range) and two or three eggs are laid. Incubation is usually by the female only, the male bringing food to her as she sits. Hatching occurs after 28–30 days, with the female brooding the young for two weeks thereafter while the male continues to supply food, after which both parents bring food to the growing chicks. The young leave the nest after 45–50 days, but remain close to the nest for two weeks.

Generally not very vocal, the main contact call is a mewing "wheee-oo" or a repeated "wee'wee'wee", sometimes extended into a rather tremulous "weee-oo'oo'oo'oo", and sounding somewhere between the Common Buzzard and Black Kite in quality. Also gives a longer, high whinnying whistle, a rising and falling "peee-ooo-weeoo-weeoo-weeoo" or "eee-oooo-eee-oooo-eee-oooo" and a plaintive "oo-eeeer". If disturbed at the nest or alarmed in other situations it will call with a repeated "peee-ee-ee-ee".

Sparrowhawk
Accipiter nisus

Length: 28–38cm

Wingspan: 55–70cm

A small raptor with a long tail, the Sparrowhawk is similar in size to the Kestrel but with short, broad blunt-tipped wings. It has a distinctive and immediately recognizable flight pattern, in level flight making several rapid flaps followed by a glide on level wings. The sexes differ strongly, both in plumage and size, the female being 25 per cent larger (and 40 per cent heavier) than the male, which is quite diminutive and roughly the size of a Mistle Thrush. The male has blue-grey upperparts, contrasting with orange-rufous on the cheeks, and with underparts that are closely barred orange-rufous on a white ground colour. The female has dark brown or slaty upperparts with brown bars on whitish underparts, and a prominent pale supercilium. Both sexes show a tail barred with four dark bands. The immature is dark-brown above, much like the female but more coarsely and irregularly marked below. In soaring flight the tail is slightly spread and the wings are held flat.

The Sparrowhawk is strongly tied to woods and forested areas, selecting both deciduous and coniferous trees for nesting, although it may be seen passing over open country, wetlands and reedbeds as it flies between wooded patches or when hunting close to the ground. It hunts by flying low and fast through patches of woodland and along forest edges, hedges and gardens,

MALE

FEMALE

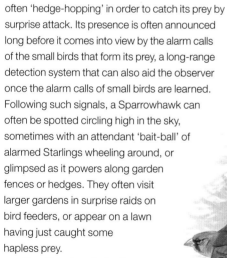

covered with white down at first, gaining feathers after two or three weeks, and leave the nest after four weeks. However, they remain dependent on their parents for an additional three or four weeks.

Only really vocal in the breeding season in the vicinity of the nest, the call being a chattering "eh!eh!eh!eh!eh!" or "kew-kew-kew-kew". It is given in a variety of situations: as a contact call between parents, rapidly by the female as an intruder-alarm call, loudly and slowly by the male as an advertising call or more quietly when it brings food for the female or chicks at the nest. Another call is a high, shrill "peeeee-peeeee-peeeee" or "wheee'wheee'wheee…", often uttered as an alarm near the nest or as a contact call from fledged young.

often 'hedge-hopping' in order to catch its prey by surprise attack. Its presence is often announced long before it comes into view by the alarm calls of the small birds that form its prey, a long-range detection system that can also aid the observer once the alarm calls of small birds are learned. Following such signals, a Sparrowhawk can often be spotted circling high in the sky, sometimes with an attendant 'bait-ball' of alarmed Starlings wheeling around, or glimpsed as it powers along garden fences or hedges. They often visit larger gardens in surprise raids on bird feeders, or appear on a lawn having just caught some hapless prey.

Breeding starts in April or May, and the nest is a fairly flat structure of twigs built mainly by the female. Four or five eggs are incubated by the female for 33 (or as many as 45) days, the male bringing food to her as she sits. The young are

ATTACKING
GREENFINCH
AT FEEDER

Buzzard
Buteo buteo

Length: 51–57cm

Wingspan: 113–128cm

This is the commonest and most widespread medium-large raptor in our region, and one that has made a remarkable expansion across Britain in recent years. It has a distinctive outline in flight, and when soaring holds its broad wings pressed forward slightly in a shallow 'V', with the short broad tail spread in a fan. It glides with wings held flat, or cruises with them cranked and angled at the carpal joint. It regularly hovers, particularly when there is little wind for soaring flight, often looking rather ungainly and awkward as it does so. In the breeding season it can be seen to rise high in the air and make swooping dives that terminate in a near stall as it sweeps upwards from the bottom of the dive; it will often combine this display with bouts of hovering. It has a compact body, thick neck and short, rounded head. The plumage can be quite variable, but typically is uniform dark brown above with a dark brown head and chest, and a lighter patch on the breast that is always paler than the brown belly or belly sides. The tail is greyish or paler brown, and adults have a darker terminal band. The carpal patches are obviously darker, the flight feathers are greyish and the primary and secondary tips are dark, forming a dark wingtip and trailing edge.

The preferred habitat is a mosaic of woodland and open areas, the former for breeding and refuge, the latter for hunting, especially over clearings, farmland, grassland, pastures and forest edge. It is often seen and heard in hilly country soaring around on warm updrafts, but also spends much time on the ground searching for earthworms. As a garden bird, it would formerly have been restricted to more rural areas, but the recent expansion means that it should be quite feasible to see it soaring over almost any airspace, attention usually being drawn by its plaintive cry.

It typically nests in a tree in woodland, either deciduous or coniferous, although it may nest on the ground – such as on a cliff or bluff – when occurring in treeless habitats such as moorland. The nest may be reused from year to year, and is a bulky structure composed of sticks and twigs with a lining of greener material, the latter constantly renewed during nesting. Breeding commences from late March through to May, with the two or three eggs incubated mainly by the female for 34–42 days. Chicks are brooded by the female for 8–12 days, with the male bringing food, following which both parents hunt, although only the female actually feeds the young. The young fly the nest after 40–50 days. It is not uncommon for smaller chicks to die or to be eaten by older siblings.

Buzzards are quite vocal, particularly in the breeding season while on their territory. A loud and plaintive disyllabic cry, "peeee'yahh" and "peeeeooh", is often uttered on the wing and also while perched. Various permutations are given in different situations, and around the nest or during courtship a very high-pitched shrill "eeee'o 'eeee'o 'eeee'o", a begging "iihp iihp iihp iihp" and a rather corvid-like "how! how!" can be heard. Generally, however, the vocabulary is limited, the lack of vocal range being compensated for by the frequent calling!

Kestrel
Falco tinnunculus

Length: 32–35cm
Wingspan: 71–80cm

A medium-small falcon with a long tail and wings, the Kestrel is the only common falcon in our region that habitually hovers (the Red-footed Falcon of eastern Europe also does so, but is only a rare visitor further west). The Kestrel fans the tail while hovering, angling the body at 45 degrees, with the head remaining immobile as it scans the ground for prey. In level flight it flaps rapidly and rather weakly, the slim body and long tail giving it a distinctive silhouette, and overall it is a much more languid flyer than other falcons. The physical characteristics of the sexes differ: the male is brick-red on the mantle and wing-coverts, with black primaries and primary coverts making a distinctive and readily identifiable upperwing pattern. The head is grey, with a weak black moustache below the eye, and the tail is grey with a broad black terminal band. The underparts are buffy and spotted black, as are the pale underwings. The female is less reddish than the male, with a brown head, browner wings, a duller black-barred tail, and overall is more spotted and barred than the male.

Resident in western Europe, and also ranging across much of Asia and Africa, it avoids dense forest, desert, barren mountains and large treeless wetlands, but can be found virtually everywhere else. An efficient and adaptable hunter, it is able to take advantage of almost every habitat, even penetrating into some urban areas and often seen hovering alongside motorways. While it may not readily drop into gardens, its relative abundance means that it may be seen in the air from gardens in many different areas.

The Kestrel utilizes a variety of nest sites, commonly nesting in a tree, either in a cavity or

MALE

FEMALE
HOVERING

in an old crow's nest or similar, or on a cliff ledge or tall building (in many European languages its name translates as 'Tower Falcon'). Breeding commences in April or May, with four or five eggs being laid. The female does most of the incubation, for 27–29 days, then broods the small chicks for two weeks while the male brings food. Both sexes will hunt once the young are feathered (at two weeks), although the female does all the actual feeding of the chicks. The young fly the nest at 27–39 days, but remain dependent on the adults for a further few weeks after that.

Like many other raptors, Kestrels are only really vocal in the breeding season and when close to the nest. The most frequently heard call is a rapid series of sharp "kee-kee-kee-kee" notes, sometimes as "kik-kik-kik" or "i'i'i'i'i'i'i", becoming sharper and shorter when excited or alarmed and often given as a threatening call when an intruder is near the nest. Other calls include a tremulous whinnying cry, "kri-ee-ee-ee-ee-ee" or "trree-r-r-r-r-eee", variable in length and intensity and used as a greeting call in courtship. It also gives a more plaintive "whee'u whee'u" and an often-repeated and sharp "kek" or "pik".

Hobby
Falco subbuteo

Length: 30–36cm

Wingspan: 82–92cm

An elegant and dashing falcon, the Hobby has long wings and a medium-long tail and is highly agile in the air, where it takes prey while on the wing. It can often be seen cruising slowly at considerable height before quickly swooping down on large flying insects; these are often then consumed on the wing, presenting a characteristic silhouette of its rather long legs stretched forward to bring the item to its head, which is bent down as it eats. The upperparts are a uniform dark blue-grey, while the underparts are creamy-white, boldly streaked black from breast to belly. The adult has plain brick-red lower belly, thighs and undertail coverts. The head pattern is striking, with a whitish throat, cheeks and half-collar, and a black mask with long and prominent black 'moustaches'. At rest the wingtips extend beyond the tail.

A summer visitor to our region, exploiting the warmer months when large flying insects are available, it favours open country with isolated trees and woods, parkland and savannah-like areas, wherever it can find a rich food source. It ranges widely while feeding, and in addition to insects (it is especially partial to dragonflies) will prey on a wide variety of small bird species, notably hirundines and even Swifts, all of which are caught on the wing. A long-distance migrant that winters in southern Africa, it can be seen in a wider variety of habitats on passage. Unless one

keer-keer-keer-keer", ascending in pitch (and often likened to the song of the Wryneck, although that is rarely heard now in Britain). Variations of this call are given in different situations, and when in alarm the call becomes more shrill and chattering, or decelerates into softer drawn-out calls, such as "ivikh! ivikh! ivikh!". It also gives a short, sharp "kipp" call, a "whit-yoo" call when high in the air and excited, and the begging call of the young is a drawn-out and urgent "peee-eh".

is lucky to have a large garden offering nesting habitat, as a garden bird it is most likely to be seen cruising high overhead in the summer sky, its presence often indicated by alarm calls from House Martins and Swallows.

For breeding it uses the nest of another species, such as Carrion Crow, either occupying an old one or appropriating a recently built structure, and often located in a small copse rather than a single isolated tree, and at some 10–20m off the ground. Breeding commences in June, and two or three eggs are laid. Incubation is typically only by the female, with the male bringing her food, for 28–29 days. The female broods the young for the first week, fed by the male, after which both sexes hunt and bring food for the young, which fledge at 28–32 days. The young birds are dependent on the adults for a short period after fledging.

The most frequently heard call, almost only ever heard near the nest, is a rather high and strangled "kew-kew-kew-kew" or "keer-

Moorhen
Gallinula chloropus

Length: 32–35cm
Wingspan: 50–55cm

One of our most familiar waterbirds, the Moorhen is smaller than the closely related Coot and has a mostly black appearance when viewed from a distance. Closer inspection reveals that it is a dark slate-grey on the neck and underparts, blacker on the head, with its most striking features being a prominent white stripe along the flanks and two white flashes on the undertail, separated centrally by black. When walking on land this latter feature becomes very prominent as the tail is flicked nervously, and the long green legs also become obvious. The upperparts are dark olive-brown, and it has a yellow-tipped red bill with a red frontal shield. The juveniles are paler and grey-brown, also with white on the undertail and along the flanks, and the throat and foreneck are whitish. Moorhens are quite arboreal, roosting in bushes and trees, and are equally at home

flying, walking or swimming, the latter with a characteristic jerking of the head and flicking of the tail.

Common and widespread, it can successfully adapt to almost any wetland habitat where dense cover exists in conjunction with freshwater, right down to the smallest dykes, ditches, ponds, slow-moving rivers and even in city parks. Although it can be very furtive, it may often be seen walking about and grazing boldly in open fields, pastures and other dry areas, but always within easy reach of cover to which it will dash when alarmed or disturbed. Gardens near water and streams are often used by feeding birds, and nesting may occur if undisturbed. They can frequently be seen on village ponds or in city parks, and wandering birds may be heard calling at night as they fly over built-up areas. The nest is a bulky platform of aquatic material built in waterside vegetation, or occasionally in a bush or tree.

The breeding season begins in March, and birds are typically double-brooded. Between 5–11 eggs are laid, with both sexes taking turns at incubation, which lasts for 9–22 days. The chicks remain in the nest for a few days after hatching, when they resemble little black balls of fluff with a red bill, before taking to the water escorted by the parents. They are able to feed alone after three weeks, and fly after six or seven weeks, although they remain close to the parents for some time. Moorhens are remarkable in that they display cooperative breeding, with the young of a first brood helping to feed the chicks of the second.

The common sound indicating the presence of this bird is a rather explosive "prrrruwk!" that is sometimes delivered in a two-syllable variant "kurr-rruck" or a higher-pitched "kirr'rr'rk". It has a variety of similarly abrupt calls, in addition to some more discreet murmuring notes, such as a quiet "pook-pook-pook" etc, and a sharp "keh-keh!", "ik'ik'ik'ik" and "kittick!", delivered in alarm. In flight it gives an "eggkh-eggkh-kehk", not dissimilar to the call of the Black-tailed Godwit and sometimes heard from wandering birds flying at night, even over urban areas.

Oystercatcher
Haematopus ostralegus

ADULT WINTER
PLUMAGE

Length: 40–46cm
Wingspan: 80–86cm

A large, bulky and strikingly coloured wader, the Oystercatcher has a long, stout, blunt-tipped, orangey-red bill used for chiselling open molluscs. It has rather stocky medium-length pink legs, and an orange-red eye-ring. The majority of the plumage is a glossy black, with a white belly and lower breast, but in flight it shows a bold and eye-catching pattern of a broad white wingbar, plus a white back and rump. In winter plumage it acquires a whitish throat strap, but otherwise changes little. Immature birds in their first winter are browner above, with a dark tip to the bill. Although quite obvious along the coast, knowledge of the loud call will greatly enhance one's chances of recording this delightful bird from the confines of a garden.

Most commonly found along coasts, where it favours shingle and pebbly beaches, seaweed-rich rocks, tidal mud, sandy flats, beaches and any intertidal areas where it can find its favourite

food of molluscs. It is also found breeding away from the coast, and has considerably increased its inland range in England in recent decades. It occurs particularly along river valleys, on lakes with suitable shingle islands, as well as in grassy fields and pastures. Outside the breeding season, concentrations build up on the coast, and there is movement of birds southwards in winter, plus immigration from further north. While not a typical garden bird, its extrovert nature and loud calls mean that it can be recorded readily from gardens, perhaps heard flying over at night or actually seen passing above during the day.

Like most shorebirds, it is a ground nester, typically laying three eggs in a shallow depression on bare ground or shingle, either unlined or with a few small stones of debris. Breeding commences in April or May, and both parents incubate the eggs for 24–27 days. On hatching, the chicks stay in the nest for just one or two days before

leaving, then following the parents but able to feed themselves. The chicks become fully fledged and independent at 34–37 days.

A noisy and obvious bird, the Oystercatcher has a range of loud and shrill piping calls, given both from the ground and also in boisterous flight activity. The common call is a "kleeep!" or a two-syllable "ke-beeep!", often heard in flight. Another commonly heard call is a sharper repeated "kip" or "keep", given excitedly in alarm when the nest or young are approached by intruders. Other calls include a higher-pitched "keeuup" and "kepiouw", often running these and the "ke-beeep" calls together with a Curlew-like trilling when in a pair or a small gathering to make a 'piping song', as in "kip'kip'kip'kip'ke-beep' ke-beep' ke-beep' kliklikliklikliklikli' krrrrrr…".

ADULT
SUMMER
PLUMAGE

Lapwing
Vanellus vanellus

Length: 28–31cm

Wingspan: 82–87cm

An unmistakable, medium-large, dumpy and long-legged plover, appearing black and white when seen at long range. The upperparts are actually a deep dark green with a purple iridescence, the underparts white, with a broad black chest band and rufous-buff undertail coverts. The head is striking, with a long thin erect crest, a black crown, forehead and lores, and in summer with a black face, chin and throat. The sides of the head and cheeks are pale grey. Immature birds are duller, with a very short crest and buff edgings to the feathers of the upperparts. It has a unique flight silhouette, with very broad blunt-tipped wings, deep wingbeats and a weak-looking or 'wobbling' flight. The underwing coverts are white, creating an alternating black/white flashing pattern when flying, most striking when a flock of birds is airborne. When feeding it will typically walk a few steps, then tilt downwards to pick up food without flexing the legs, in typical plover fashion.

In the breeding season and throughout the year it can be found on

grasslands, meadows, pastures, lakesides and the margins of marshes, as well as on arable fields where vegetation is not too high. In winter they will flock on to arable land, saltmarshes and other tidal habitats. Lapwings require a degree of dampness in the substrate and a richness of invertebrate food, and will avoid hard and arid ground where feeding is difficult. Large numbers of immigrants arrive in Britain from mainland Europe in winter, and Lapwings can often be seen in flight, travelling to and from feeding and roosting areas, at which time they may be seen from any garden with a good vantage point.

It lays four eggs in a shallow hollow, either bare or with a small accumulation of vegetation, and often on a slight prominence in otherwise flat and open country. The male will prepare several scrapes, from which the female will choose one, and breeding commences in late March until June, depending on latitude. Incubation is mostly done by the female, for 25–34 days, and the chicks will leave the nest shortly after hatching. They are tended by both parents, with the female largely leading and brooding while the male does most of the guarding. The young are independent after 33–40 days.

An old common English name related to the call is 'Peewit'. They are very vocal, either conversationally when in a flock or on the breeding grounds, where they create a lot of noise if alarmed. In spring they make a tumbling and dive-bombing display flight, accompanied by a more elaborate call sequence or 'song', "whee'wheedle-wi'up'ee-wip'ee-wip'ee-wip'iyuweeep!", along with a low throbbing sound that emanates from the vigorous wingbeats. The commonly heard call at all seasons is a "whheee'ow", "eeeee'woah", an ascending "wheeeo-wheep!" or a lower and hoarser "eeoo-whep". Slight variations of this call are given depending on their state of anxiety, the alarm note being a shriller and more urgent "eeeeo'whip!"

Woodcock
Scolopax rusticola

Length: 33–35cm
Wingspan: 45–51cm

A very plump and medium-sized wader with broad rounded wings and a long bill for probing in soft mud. The legs are short, and the eyes are set very high in the head, giving it 360-degree vision. The plumage is very cryptic, with reddish-brown upperparts intricately barred and marbled with black, white and buff, and dark-barred buff underparts, giving the effect of 'dead leaf' camouflage. The face is rather pale and plain, and the crown is patterned with broad blackish transverse bars. In addition to being very well camouflaged, it is crepuscular and secretive, and therefore usually only encountered when 'roding' (see below) or when flushed. It takes to the air with a clatter and swiftly gets away, weaving through the trees and bushes and dropping down into cover again fairly quickly.

Throughout the year it can be found in deciduous, coniferous and mixed forests with some undergrowth and shade, especially when soft boggy ground, streams and pools are present. It sometimes also nests in more open areas on bracken-rich moorland. It is resident in western Europe, with birds from further north

'RODING'
FLIGHT

and east supplementing the resident British population in winter, when they can be found in scrub, urban cemeteries, reedbeds and thickets. This is the season when they are most likely to be seen in gardens, sometimes probing a lawn or soil with their long bill or, more likely, flushed off the ground on clattering wings. When 'roding' in spring and summer, they fly around a wide circuit just above treetop height and therefore may be visible from rural gardens that are close to breeding habitat.

Nesting commences in March, in a shallow scrape lined with dead leaves and often placed close to a tree. They are double-brooded, and four eggs are laid in each clutch. The female alone incubates for 21–24 days, with the chicks ready to leave the nest very soon after hatching and tended solely by the female. They are able to fly a little after two weeks, are fully fledged after three, and independent after five. When in danger, the female may carry her chicks clasped between her thighs as she flies away, and one has even been recorded carrying a chick under her wing. With these birds so hard to see at the best of times, the sight of a female

Woodcock carrying her young must rate as one of the rarest and most exciting encounters of all.

Woodcock are not particularly vocal, except on the breeding grounds, when males perform a display flight known as 'roding'. They patrol their woodland territories and beyond, often just above treetop height, flying level with a jerky action and stiff rapid wingbeats, bill pointing down at 45 degrees. During this circuit they regularly utter a strange combination of sounds, the most audible being a high-pitched and far-carrying (3–14kHz)"SpiSSp!", but at closer range low (0.6–1.5kHz) croaking notes can be heard preceding this sneezing call, as in "wurr'urr'urr'rr'SpiSSp!". With a good close view, the bird can be seen to jerk its legs in time to the rhythm! Little-known calls occur between the sexes when on the ground, such as "bibibibibib", plus the female may call down the roding male with a softer and quieter version of his roding sneeze, "iiiitz-iiiitz psit". Birds chasing each other around may give a "plip'plip'pissp'psi'plip". The only call that seems to be heard at all seasons is a Snipe-like "scaap", given in flight.

Black-headed Gull

Larus ridibundus

Length: 34–37cm
Wingspan: 100–110cm

ADULT
SUMMER
PLUMAGE

The familiar small gull in our region. The adult in summer has a chocolate-brown (not black) head, and shows various transitional states between this and the winter plumage of a white head with just a dark smudge over the eye and a bold dark ear-spot. The upperparts are pearly grey, with a long white wedge from the primary coverts to the outer primary tips, a black trailing edge to the primaries and smoky grey underside to the flight feathers. Immature birds take two years to mature, and are blotched and marked with dark brown in decreasing amounts with age, but always have a roughly similar pattern of black and white on the primaries as the adult.

Common throughout our region and fairly ubiquitous in most wetland habitats. It breeds on a variety of open areas close to water, both coastally and inland, in a raucous colony that is unlikely to go unnoticed. Outside the breeding season Black-headed Gulls are found even more

WINTER
PLUMAGE

widely, in urban areas, parks, playing fields, sewage farms, rubbish tips, reservoirs, inlets, estuaries and intertidal areas. They are a familiar sight around towns and villages, where they will cruise around, foraging and scavenging wherever they can find food, and often appearing from nowhere to swoop down on scraps (bread and chips seem to be particular favourites) thrown out by householders. They infrequently land in small enclosed areas, being nervous of places where their airspace is restricted, but are otherwise easy to lure in with food as they hover to pick up any suitable morsels, or even catch them in mid-air. They are noisy when coming to food, squabbling and screeching until the food is depleted, after which they quietly disperse.

Nesting occurs from April to July around shallow brackish and saline marshy pools, lakes, gravel pits, reedbeds, saltmarshes, estuaries, broad slow-moving rivers and flooded areas. Birds often favour small shingly islands for security but also use drier areas close to water, such as heather moors and dunes. The nest is a shallow scrape carelessly lined with vegetable matter, in which two to three eggs are laid and incubated by both sexes for 23–26 days. A short time after hatching the chicks leave the nest but remain in its vicinity, being tended by both parents until able to fly, which occurs after five or six weeks.

It is very vocal, particularly around breeding colonies where the noise can be deafening and often continues through the night. It has a variety of rather unattractive harsh calls, the commonest of which is a downwards-inflected screech "krreearr" or "kaa'aarrr". It also gives a harsher and insistent "raaargh!" or "gaaarhh!" when reacting anxiously to the presence of intruders. A softer and less urgent "aaarrrr", "akh'akh'akh", and singles and multiples of "kik", are all delivered in a more conversational tone. A longer and more elaborate call, "kre-kre-kreh'kraaa'kraaaa'kraaaa'kraaaa", is given in various social contexts.

1ST WINTER PLUMAGE

Common Gull
Larus canus

Length: 40–42cm
Wingspan: 110–120cm

WINTER ADULTS
AND 1ST WINTER

A very handsome medium-sized gull, superficially similar to the Herring Gull but intermediate between that species and Black-headed Gull in both size and structure. It has a white head, streaked dusky in winter, with a dark eye, a gentle expression and a greenish-yellow bill. The legs are also greenish-yellow, and the wings are long, with a large amount of black on the primary tips and a large white panel or 'mirror' on the very tip. The mantle and upperwings are a mid-grey with a smoky-bluish tone. In their first juvenile plumage they have a neat pattern of dark-centred, pale-fringed mantle feathers that is lost in the first winter. They take three years to reach maturity, and in their first year show dark brown on the upperwing coverts and on the underwing, plus more extensive black on the primaries. Immature head markings are as for the winter adult, and the amounts of dark brownish markings on the head and body decrease as they gradually mature into adult plumage. The legs and base of the bill are pinkish in immature birds.

During the breeding season it is found around marshes, lakes, bogs, grassy moorland, in coastal

IMMATURE

ADULT

and island habitats, dunes, grassy and rocky slopes, along broad river valleys with shingle banks, and occasionally on cliffs, roofs and other elevated situations. After breeding, and in winter, birds disperse onto grassland and farmland, often following the plough, and can be found in a wider range of wetland and dry country, such as reservoirs, gravel pits, playing fields, parks, pastures, flooded areas, and coastally in harbours and on estuaries and sandy beaches. Frequently seen on school sports fields, they have a habit of paddling on the spot, which probably mimics the patter of rain and encourages worms to come to the surface. It is less likely to be seen around city streets and urban areas than the Black-headed Gull, although it can be lured with food if foraging nearby. Often seen overhead when flying to roost on winter afternoons and evenings.

Breeding occurs from May to July, either colonially or singly, and the nest is a shallow scrape built by the female, with a variable amount of interior decoration and nest lining. Three eggs are laid and are incubated by both sexes for 22–28 days. After hatching the chicks stay close to the nest and are tended by both parents until they are able to fly at five weeks.

The calls are higher-pitched than those of the Herring Gull but it has a similar range of vocalizations, with a whining, mewing quality which gives it the alternative name of 'Mew Gull'. The long call is a shrill nasal "eh'eh'eh'eh'wheeeee-yow wheeee-yow wheee-yow ee'ya ee'ya ee'ya'eh'eh", with variants such as "aah-ow aa-ow ar'ar'ar'ar'ar" and an excited "wheeyah-wheeyah-wheeyah-wheeyah'wow". These calls are uttered in flight or on the ground, when it stretches the head back and up. Various shorter calls are given, such as a rather knowing "raow!" or "arrrw!", or sharper yelps such as "arr!" and "yaow!", often then breaking into longer sequences of shrill mewing calls.

Lesser Black-backed Gull

Larus fuscus

Length: 52–64cm

Wingspan: 135–150cm

JUVENILE

A common sight over much of Britain, both coastally and inland. Typically a little smaller, slimmer and more graceful than the Herring Gull, the adult *graellsii* form found in Britain has a dark slate-grey back and upperwings, rather extensive black wingtips and a small white 'mirror' on the outer primary tips. The head is white, becoming blotched and streaked in winter. The Scandinavian forms *intermedius* and *fuscus* have very black upperparts, resembling the Great Black-backed Gull, but all forms show yellow legs and a smaller and more slender bill than the Great. Immatures take four years to mature, and in their first year are fairly densely and uniformly patterned, with blackish on brown on the upperparts and whitish-brown on the underparts and body. The adult plumage is acquired gradually, and from their second year birds begin to

resemble adults, but with the white parts streaked and blotched and the grey upperside variably patterned with brown.

Until relatively recently, the Lesser Black-backed Gull was mainly a summer visitor to our region, wintering in France and Portugal, but nowadays a rapidly increasing number stay in Britain for the winter, and they have become a common sight in many areas. During the breeding

ADULT

season they favour grassy areas on low or rocky islands, sea cliffs, coastal dunes, as well as inland on moorland, bogs, lakes and increasingly on buildings in urban areas. Outside the breeding season birds disperse widely, over offshore and inshore waters such as lagoons, estuaries, harbours, shorelines and tidal areas, reservoirs, gravel pits, flooded pasture, ploughed fields, farmland, urban areas and sports fields. Non-breeding birds may be seen inland throughout the summer months, and this species can be observed easily from many gardens as birds forage over urban areas or fly to roost on inland water bodies. It avoids confined airspace, but will come to food scraps provided it can easily manoeuvre its 1½-metre wingspan in and out.

It typically nests colonially in habitat similar to the Herring Gull. Breeding occurs from May to July, and the nest is a shallow scrape on the ground lined with plant material. Three eggs are laid and incubated by both sexes for 24–27 days, and after hatching the young remain close to the nest and are tended by both parents for 30–40 days.

The various calls are similar in pattern to those of both the Herring and Great Black-backed Gulls. The 'long-call' is deeper and more nasal than that of the Herring, as in "rru'rru'rru'rru'rru'rru…" or "egh-egh-egh-egh-egh…", and may accelerate towards the end of the sequence. It also has a barking anxiety call, "gow'ow'ow'ow'ow", deeper and gruffer than the Herring. The simple calls are a nasal descending "eeeyhhr" or "ehrrw", or a repeated "owrr owrr owrr", all lower in pitch than those of the Herring. It also has a more plaintive, slightly higher-pitched "i'i'i'errr" or "oo-eeerrr", given by juveniles.

Herring Gull
Larus argentatus

Length: 56–64cm

Wingspan: 138–150cm

JUVENILE

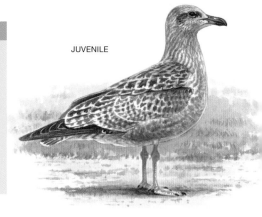

The most familiar large 'seagull' in our region, with a pale grey back and upperwings, a white head (variably streaked in winter), pink legs and a yellow bill with a red spot on the lower mandible near the tip. The wingtips are black with white tips and a white 'mirror' spanning the tips of the two outermost primaries. The iris is pale yellow. Young birds take four years to mature, and in their first year are rather uniformly blotched and barred pale brown, with the feathers of the wing and mantle well marked with black bars and centres. As they mature further, the mantle and wings gradually moult out the brown feathers and acquire grey ones, until they reach the neat grey plumage of adulthood in their fourth year.

A common bird, typically breeding in coastal areas (but occasionally far inland), with a preference for sea cliffs and rocky coasts, as well as islands, dunes and moorland. Outside the breeding season it frequents similar habitats, but also ranges more widely onto arable fields and farmland, harbours, bays, estuaries and saltmarshes, always keeping within range of large waterbodies for roosting, such as reservoirs and lakes, and usually never too far from the coast. Successful and adaptable, it takes

ADULT

ADULT AND IMMATURES WITH
LESSER BLACK-BACKED GULL

advantage of human food refuse, scavenging from fishing boats, markets, docks and rubbish tips. In coastal localities this can be a regular 'garden bird' (particularly visible if bread is thrown), but can also be seen over urban areas country-wide. Less numerous inland than Lesser Black-backed Gulls, they can still be found on playing fields and other open grassy areas, or seen flying to roost in small flocks.

It will often nest on buildings in coastal towns and ports, a habit that has only developed since the 1920s. The nest is built by both sexes and is a bulky mass of grass and seaweed in a hollow, with breeding occurring from late April until July. Three eggs are laid, with incubation by both sexes but primarily by the female, and lasting for 28–30 days. The young are brooded for the first few days after hatching, and following this do not stray far from the nest. They are tended by both adults and fledge after 35–40 days.

Quite vocal, especially during the breeding season, with their calls representing the classic sound of the seaside. The simple and familiar call is a high ringing "eeow!" or "kyaow", often heard as a medley of cries when several birds are present. Variants include a rather high-pitched "eeoow!", sometimes an "eeuurrw!" in a lower pitch or a shorter and sharper "kliu", etc. A rather deep barking "og'og'og'og" is given in anxiety, also a softer, less worried "ah'ah'ah'ow". The long call is "eeo'eeo'eeo'eeoo'eeoo'eeoo'eu'eu'argh'argh'ar gh'aa-ow'aa-ow", delivered in a display sequence where the neck stretches down to the ground, is then pulled inwards and slowly raised upwards before relaxing. While gull-haters may disagree, (perhaps understandably fed up with being woken in the early hours by the raucousness!) the sound of the Herring Gull has been proposed as the most powerful, evocative and indeed most beautiful of all British bird sounds.

Rock Dove & Feral Pigeon

Columba livia

Length: 31–34cm

Wingspan: 63–70cm

The familiar 'town pigeon' has been with mankind for a very long time. Today's birds, with their highly variable plumage, are the descendants of wild Rock Doves, previously cultivated for food in large dovecotes or bred as racing pigeons. The original plumage of the Rock Dove is an attractive combination of greys; pale grey on the wing coverts and mantle, darker grey on the head, neck and breast, and with two bold black wingbars or 'straps' across the wings. It shows an iridescent green-and-purple patch on the side of its neck, and is distinct from other pigeons in having a white-rump (although some populations lack this); the tail is mid-grey with a narrow black terminal band. The underwing is white with a narrow black border, a feature that sets it apart from both the Woodpigeon and Stock Dove. It has a conspicuously fast and dashing flight, much more so than most of its relatives, and also wheels and glides effortlessly, being totally at home in the air.

Really wild Rock Doves have decreased drastically and are absent from England and Wales, with colonies persisting only in remote coastal regions of Scotland, Ireland and the

wildest corners of northern Europe, although how much mixing there has been of wild birds with their feral congeners is often hard to gauge. They are found around sea cliffs and in caves, gorges and on suitable rock faces in mountainous areas. Despite the famed homing abilities over long distances of racing pigeons, Rock Doves are usually sedentary. Feral Pigeons are often abundant in towns and cities, and are a common sight in the centre of urban areas, strutting about on pavements.

Feral Pigeons nest on the ledges of buildings and bridges high off the ground, as well as inside derelict buildings and in any niche that provides a suitable nesting space, so long as it is not too far from drinking water and bathing places. The display flight is not dissimilar to that of the Woodpigeon, with a

swooping flight accompanied by wing claps. The nest is made of a variable amount of local vegetation or litter, and breeding occurs from March to September. Two eggs are laid and incubated by both sexes for 16–19 days. The young are brooded continually at first, and fed by both parents. They can fly at five weeks.

This is a bird with a limited vocal repertoire and no contact calls or calls given in flight. The common and familiar 'hoo' calls are the territorial advertising calls of the male. He gives a rolling, moaning "u'u'u'uh'ohrwrrr" or a shorter 'uh'owrrr", also rendered as "ooohrrrr" or "ohh-oo-oor" and repeated several times. Females give a variant of this call that is hoarser and softer, and when a pair are together they give some more hurried and excited guttural sounds as part of their sexual attraction display.

Stock Dove
Columba oenas

Length: 32–34cm
Wingspan: 63–69cm

Arguably the most handsome of the pigeons, this dapper bird is rather subtle and easily overlooked owing to its superficial similarity to the more familiar Rock Dove/Feral Pigeon and Woodpigeon. It is dumpy and compact, and shorter-tailed than its close relatives, with a darker, bluer, more uniform plumage that shows no white on the rump or wing. In flight it is fast and direct, showing black trailing and leading edges to the primaries, which give a black frame to the bluish wings. It has a broad black tail band, a vinaceous wash on the breast and on its neck there is a metallic flash of shimmering green and lilac.

A rather shy and discreet bird, the Stock Dove favours open deciduous woodland and forest edge, large parklands and mature hedgerows, occupying the narrow interface between woodland and open country and most frequently seen around arable land. It is fairly dependent on finding suitable nest holes and hollows in large old trees such as oaks, and also requires access to feeding areas in fields that are rich in weeds and seed crops, open bare ground where it can feed, and accessible drinking water. While Stock Doves are unlikely to be encountered in inner city gardens, they may appear in gardens in close proximity to suitable habitat, either coming down to feed on spilt seed, perched up in nearby large trees, or perhaps foraging on a sports field.

Breeding occurs from March through to September, and occasionally several birds will nest in a loose colony. Most pairs nest in holes in trees, but locally they will breed on cliffs and in quarries in rock crevices, as well as in buildings when suitable trees are absent, with nests quite often found inside derelict barns and outhouses. Two eggs are laid in a hollow, with variable amounts of nest lining, and

both sexes take turns at incubation, which lasts for 21–23 days. The young remain in the nest for 28–29 days. There are two, and sometimes three, broods.

The most frequently heard call is the advertising call, a deep two-note sound "ooo-wuhh, ooo-wuhh, ooo-wuhh…", the first syllable longer and higher pitched, the second lower and sounding as though the note is being swallowed, repeated eight or nine times in a series. This is often heard in spring, coming from large woodland trees but is easily overlooked. Another similar call is given by the male in display to the female, a more drawn-out and low-pitched "uuh'whurrr uuh'whurrr". In the display flight the male flies horizontally with slow deep wingbeats, clapping the wingtips over its back, followed by a sweeping glide.

Woodpigeon
Columba palumbus

Length: 40–42cm
Wingspan: 75–80cm

The largest of our pigeons, a very plump and heavy bird with a small head and medium-long tail. It is light blue-grey all over, with a prominent white patch on the side of the neck. The flight feathers are black and contrast with the grey wing coverts, which are bisected by a prominent white transverse bar on the upperwing which is mostly obscured at rest. The tail has a greyish-white subterminal band and a broad black terminal band. The deep chest is washed purplish-pink. Woodpigeons can appear rather long-necked, particularly when craning to reach seed feeders that are supposed to provide for sparrows and finches!

Very common and even abundant in many places, the population has undergone a steady and steep increase since at least the mid-1970s. They can be found in parks, gardens and urban areas, forests, small scattered or fragmented woodlands, and particularly in agricultural areas and fields where they often feed in huge flocks.

platform in a tree or bush, often flimsy enough for the eggs to be seen from below through the twigs. Two eggs are laid and incubated by both parents for 17 days, and following hatching the squabs are fed by both sexes and fledge after 33–34 days. Pigeons feed their young a 'milk' formed from sloughing off fluid-filled cells in the crop lining, which is apparently more nutritious than human or cow's milk. As a garden bird, they are a fairly universal, if not always popular, addition to the bird table, dominating and bullying through their sheer size and apparent clumsiness. Pigeons thrive on the wheat and other seeds contained within cheaper versions of mixed birdseed and which are thrown aside by small birds, which are more selective about what they eat.

The commonly heard song is one of the classic sounds of the summer months, and is given from early spring through to autumn. It is a deep, five-syllable "wooh-oooo, wor-ooh, woh-WHOOR-ooh, wor-hoo, woh-WHOOR-ooh, wor-hoo, wu-WHOOR-ooh, wor-hoo", repeated three to five times, and often finished with a short upward-inflected "whu!" Another call is given by the male in a bowing display towards the female, a low growling "whu'-oorr", repeated at intervals. The familiar display flight consists of a short steep climb, at the apex of which the bird delivers several loud wing claps, before gliding back down. When disturbed, birds will make a lot of wing clapping and clattering noises on take-off, which functions as an alarm call.

British birds are resident, but large numbers of immigrants arrive for the winter from northern and eastern parts of Europe, and can be seen in large numbers at migration watchpoints. The spread of intensive arable cultivation (oilseed rape in particular) has been shown to promote winter survival rates, which may explain the rise in numbers. It has also been established that the Woodpigeon breeding season has advanced in response to the switch to autumn sowing, and thus earlier ripening, of cereals, with more pairs nesting in May and June and relatively fewer in July–September.

They nest almost anywhere, even in towns, the male bringing twigs for the female to fashion a

Collared Dove
Streptopelia decaocto

Length: 31–33cm
Wingspan: 47–55cm

The Collared Dove is a relatively rare phenomenon – a bird that has naturally and emphatically colonized Britain. It is now common and even abundant in many areas, particularly in gardens, and their soft cooing has become part of the suburban soundscape.

In fact, before 1955 it had never even been recorded in this country, yet in that year it arrived at Cromer in Norfolk and started breeding, part of a remarkable expansion of its range in southeast Europe, from where the population spread northwestwards from the 1930s onwards. It has since colonized all of Britain up to Shetland, has reached the Faeroe Islands and even Iceland, and also now breeds quite far north in Scandinavia.

A medium-sized dove, it is much more slender and elegant than the Woodpigeon, weighing just 40 per cent of the most well-fed examples of that species. Overall it is a pallid greyish-buff mushroom colour, with a browner cast to the back and wings. It has an obvious black half-collar, a beady eye, grey flight feathers and a pale blue-grey panel on the greater coverts. The tail is quite long, with a broad white terminal band on all but the central feathers.

In western Europe, and indeed throughout much of its range, it is commonest in urban and suburban areas, utilizing habitats such as gardens,

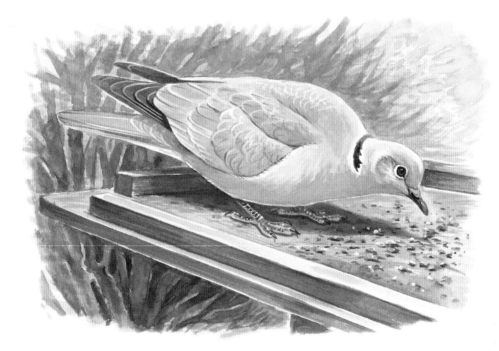

both sexes for 16–17 days, and both parents feed the chicks until they leave the nest after 17–19 days. It can raise three broods a year, and sometimes as many as five. A very vocal dove that sings throughout much of the year, yet its vocal range is limited. The commonly heard advertising call is a trisyllabic hollow cooing, with the first syllable a little higher in pitch and somewhat more emphatic, the second syllable also emphatic but the longest of the three notes in duration, the third syllable being shorter and rather 'swallowed', as in "Ooh'OOO-oo Ooh'OOO-oo Ooh'OOO-oo...". It has one other commonly heard call, a rather thin and nasal "eerrrrr" or "rrrrrehh", given in excitement, in flight and upon alighting. It also produces noisy wing flaps when flushed.

parks, churchyards and orchards, as well as farmyards. A seed-eater, it has benefited greatly from garden seed feeders, clearing up the grain that spills onto the ground below. It can be found wherever there are a few dense trees together with numerous perches such as telephone poles and wires. In the core of its range in India it is a bird of drier habitats, found even in semi-desert.

It builds a thin platform of a nest in a tree (or more rarely on a ledge), constructed of fine twigs and stems. Two eggs are laid and incubated by

Turtle Dove
Streptopelia turtur

Length: 26–28cm
Wingspan: 47–53cm

A slim dove with fairly long, pointed wings and a dashing and swift flight action. The most obvious plumage feature is the bright, black-centred, orange-rufous feathers on the mantle and lesser coverts, with a pale grey-blue panel on the greater coverts. The throat and breast are vinous-pink, and the head and neck are pale ashy-grey. The belly and undertail are white, contrasting with the dark grey underwings, a useful identification feature when it flies overhead. It has a bold pattern on the side of the neck of five bluish-white bars interspersed with four black bars. The tail is boldly marked, with a white terminal band, a black subterminal band on the upperside, and more extensively black on the underside. It also has a patch of bare, dark red skin surrounding the eye.

Our only transcontinental migrant dove, it is a summer visitor that spends the winter in sub-Saharan Africa. It favours dry, sunny, sheltered lowlands, breeding in open deciduous woodlands with rich undergrowth, open country with mature hedges and scattered trees, copses and forest edge, commonly around cultivated areas with dry open patches. Much decreased in Britain in the last two decades, and unfortunately still heavily hunted while on passage through Mediterranean countries. Generally shy in its habits and avoiding human habitation, it may appear in undisturbed gardens in suburban and rural areas when these are in proximity to its preferred habitats and it can take advantage of spilt seed on the ground or on bird tables. In coastal gardens migrants may be seen pausing for rest or just passing through, as they undertake their spring and autumn migration during the hours of daylight.

Breeding occurs between May and July, the nest being built by the female as a flimsy platform of twigs with a scanty lining

TURTLE DOVE WITH
COLLARED DOVES

of stems and roots. Two eggs are incubated by both sexes for 15–16 days, the chicks are fed by both parents and fledge after 1 –19 days. There are usually two broods.

The song of the Turtle Dove, one of the most evocative sounds of a summer's day in the countryside, is traditionally described as a 'tur-tur', as per the scientific name. It is a deep, hard purring sound, typically in three- (although often just two-) syllable phrases, repeated for 3–12 phrases at a time. The longer first syllable rises slightly, while the others are level, as in "crrrrrr 'orrr 'orrr', crrrrrr 'orrr 'orrr', crrrrrr 'orrr 'orrr', crrrrr 'orrr 'orrr", or "rrrrrr-rrrr-rrr" etc. It can also give a faster, more

hurried version of this song, delivered by the male directly towards the female in a bobbing display. It also has a short popping call given in excitement.

Rose-ringed Parakeet

Psittacula krameri

Length: 38–42cm

Wingspan: 42–48cm

An unmistakable addition to the British avifauna, this noisy bird has become abundant in some areas of south-east England after being introduced and first breeding in Kent in 1969. A native of southern Asia and sub-Saharan Africa, the British population was recently estimated at 30,000 birds, with further feral populations existing in Germany and the Low Countries.

It has a 25cm-long wedge-shaped tail, giving the bird a long, tapering shape while in flight,

which is typically powerful, direct and rapid. It is a uniform pale green, with a blue sheen on the tail and rear of the crown. The bird takes its name from the male's collar of rosy red on the hind-neck, which connects with a black throat and collar at the front. The female has a plain green head with just a hint of a blue hind-collar. The bill is orange with a strongly curved upper mandible. The flight feathers are darker and contrast with the rest of the plumage when in flight.

In its native range, it favours lightly wooded country and open lowland forest. Feral birds in Europe are usually found in open woodlands, leafy suburban areas, parks and large gardens. Garden feeders are an important source of food for British populations, and they frequently visit gardens in search of food. They form large and very noisy roost gatherings, not always welcome in residential areas!

In Britain breeding takes place between January and June, using a hole in a tree, either a natural cavity or an old woodpecker hole that may then be enlarged by the female parakeet. Three or four eggs are laid and incubated by the female for 22–24 days. The chicks are brooded almost continuously when small, and are fed by both parents. Fledging occurs after 40–50 days.

The vocal range is rather limited, but is more than made up for by volume! The typically heard call is a screeching "kee-yak, kee-yak, kee-yak" or "kyaak-kyaak-kyaak", given either from a perch or in flight. It also gives a descending "kheek-keek-keek", with the emphasis on the first syllable. Various other, less strident, calls can be heard, with the female making some soft twittering and chuckling sounds and the male giving subdued but high-pitched whistling and warbling notes, such as an enquiring "kiier" and a sharp "kihk".

Common Cuckoo
Cuculus canorus

Length: 32–34cm
Wingspan: 55–60cm

HEPATIC
FEMALE

A slim, rakish bird with a superficial similarity to a small falcon, its pointed wings and long rounded tail giving it a distinctive silhouette in flight as it beats its wings rapidly below the body without gliding until just prior to perching when it glides in to land. When perched and calling, it typically droops the long wingtips below the body. It has a small rounded head and small thin bill, and is uniformly grey on the head, breast and upperparts, while the underparts are white with regular fine black bands on the belly. Rufous or 'hepatic' morphs occur only in the female, and are a rusty-red barred with black, the belly being white barred with black.

A summer migrant. it arrives from Africa in April, with the adults returning in July and August and the juveniles following on during August and September. It is found in a very wide range

NESTLING WITH
DUNNOCK HOST

of habitats, typically in wooded areas, scrub, open country with hedges and scattered trees, reedbeds and wetland margins. It can be found in gardens with suitable habitat, but is perhaps more often just heard as it passes nearby or overhead. Its only real requirement is to have song perches within the habitat of any of the 100 different possible host species that have been recorded as being 'nest-parasitized'. Common hosts in Britain include Meadow Pipit, Dunnock, Reed and Sedge Warblers, Pied Wagtail and Robin.

Needless to say, it does not build a nest or take part in any kind of chick rearing, all the work being done by other species on its behalf! The female will fly back and forth over bushes or reeds etc, watching for any brooding target species that may shoot off the nest on its approach, fooled into this response by the Cuckoo's raptor-like appearance. Breeding begins in May, and female Cuckoos will lay 12 or more eggs per season. One egg is laid in the nest of each host, and the Cuckoo will remove one of the host bird's eggs already present. Hatching occurs after 12.5 days, and the young Cuckoo chick will then eject the other eggs or chicks from the nest by heaving them over the edge with its back. The chick can fly after 20–23 days, but may continue being fed by the hapless foster parents. The Cuckoo is truly one of nature's marvels. Young Cuckoos probably never meet adults of their species on the breeding grounds, yet all of the information they need – the song, the breeding strategies, the migration to and from Africa etc – are all hard-wired into the egg.

The song is widely recognized and gives the bird its name in many languages. It is sung by the male in the breeding season, from a perch as well as in flight, to advertise his occupancy of territory. It is a disyllabic "HAK-koo HAK-koo HAK-koo...", the first syllable being higher pitched than the second. This is repeated in long sequences, sometimes at night, and in Britain is typically heard from the birds' arrival in April until June. There is also a variant, in which the first syllable is repeated two or three times, as in "hak-hak-hak-koo", and it is not uncommon to hear a songster with what sounds like a sore throat, emitting a strangled croak instead of the full note. Females have a bright liquid bubbling call, not dissimilar to the call of the Little Grebe, lasting for a couple of seconds. Another call given is a harsh "gowk", often repeated, and juveniles can be noisy with a piercing "chiz-chiz-chiz".

MALE

Barn Owl
Tyto alba

Length: 33–35cm
Wingspan: 85–93cm

A medium-sized owl with a slim body, long broad wings, and longish legs, which are often dangled in flight. The heart-shaped facial disc is white, and the eyes are black. The underparts and underwing are pure white, with the upperwing and remainder of the upperparts marbled pale grey on pale yellow-buff. A rare visitor to Britain is the continental race *guttata*, also known as 'Dark-breasted Barn Owl', which has a variable amount of rich buff on the underparts, making the white face even more prominent. Its upperparts are predominantly ash-grey on a golden-buff ground, hence appearing much darker above than with the resident *alba* race. Barn Owls in flight appear ghostly, and can often be seen hunting in a slow and measured fashion, low over the ground, hovering briefly before dropping on to prey. They are often seen hunting in daylight, particularly on long summer evenings or during short winter days, and have an upright stance when perched. They are vulnerable to being

hit by cars owing to their habit of hunting low along verges.

The Barn Owl has a huge worldwide range, and is widespread in Europe. After a period of decline, numbers in Britain now appear to have stabilized and, although still rather localized, it is not uncommon.

It favours open country with scattered trees, farmland mixed with small woods, hedges, scrub, margins of wetlands and areas with rough grass and herbage cover that provide a ready supply of mice and other prey, also ranging over

saltmarshes and other open habitats outside the breeding season. It will occur in or over gardens adjacent to suitable habitat, and can also be induced to nest within a large garden if nest boxes are provided.

As the name suggests, it nests in barns, as well as haystacks, roofs, old buildings, undisturbed outhouses, ruins, cliffs and quarries, often using nest boxes placed within buildings as well as old or dead trees with large cavities. Breeding usually commences in May, with four to six eggs laid at two-day intervals and incubated by the female. They hatch after 32 days and the chicks are tended and fed by both parents. However, the chicks vary in size and in lean times

the smallest may get eaten by its siblings. They can fly the nest after 60 days.

It has a variety of unique screeching and rasping sounds that sound eerie and perturbing when heard for the first time. The typical call, given by the female, is a rising and high-pitched rasp "ekhhhhrrrrrr!" or a higher-pitched "iiiiieeeeeee". Another similar call is a "ssschhhhhhhhh…" not unlike steam being forced out of a small aperture. The advertising call or song of the male, often given in flight, is a little more rolling, with a liquid gargling quality, "iiirrrrrrr"r'r'r'r'rl!". Young birds in the nest can be quite noisy, making snoring and vowel-less rasping 'ghosts in the attic' noises, such as "hhhkhkhkhkh…".

Little Owl
Athene noctua

Length: 21–23cm

Wingspan: 54–58cm

An endearing small and compact owl, with a broad, rounded head and distinctive scowling expression. It is mid-brown all over, with whitish underparts heavily streaked brown and plainer brown upperparts with some large and irregular white spots, mainly on the scapulars and wing coverts. It has prominent whitish eyebrows that may reach the nape, where it shows a rearwards-facing 'false face', a distinctive characteristic when seen from the rear. It has piercing yellow eyes, but lacks the clearly defined dark facial disc present in other owl species. It stands rather erect on longish legs, and often bobs when suspicious or agitated, bowing and straightening its body excitedly. The flight is usually low and in a bounding action in a manner not dissimilar to a woodpecker, but when hunting it flies directly at its target.

Introduced into Britain from continental Europe in the late nineteenth century, the Little Owl has spread across England and Wales. It favours open country and farmland with scattered

trees, quarries, hedges, copses, orchards and parkland, especially where old trees or farm buildings are available to provide roosting and nesting cavities, as well as plenty of perching posts. It can also be found in marginal habitats such as around cliffs, quarries, moorland and waste ground, but avoids dense vegetation and wet areas, preferring drier terrain. It is regularly encountered in the daytime, sitting on posts, buildings or in big old trees with bare branches, and often basking in the sun close to the nest during the breeding season. Most hunting is done at dawn and dusk, however.

Breeding commences in April, and the nest is in a natural hole in a tree, wall or similar, without any nest material. Three or four eggs are laid and incubated by the female for 29–31 days. The young are tended by both parents, and fly after 35 days. It may often be seen around more rural gardens if big old trees are present, although it does not generally use nest boxes.

Quite vocal at dusk, when it uses a shrill, disyllabic, sharply descending contact call "ii!'poh" or "keiw-ho!", with a higher first syllable and a lower-pitched second syllable, vaguely similar to a shortened Curlew call. The advertising call of the male is a clear whistling and rather mournful hoot, again a disyllabic sound but with the second syllable rising and higher pitched than the longer first syllable, as in "U'aaaoo-uh!" or "aaaaa-uh!", repeated every 5–10 seconds. The female can give a version of this call that is flatter and less inflected, such as "Aooo-oo". Other calls are an emphatic, forced-sounding "wheow!" or "wheee'u", a wheezy "thup thup", and an alarm call of repeated sharp wheezy notes, "shi'shi'shi'shi'shi'shi" or "ik'ik'ik'ik…".

Tawny Owl
Strix aluco

Length: 37–39cm
Wingspan: 94–104cm

A medium-sized, broad-winged owl with a dumpy, hunched shape and large rounded head. The 'bark-camouflage' plumage is very cryptic, being brown all over and mottled or variegated with darker markings, and with paler brown-streaked underparts. It shows two obvious pale stripes on the crown, and some pale spotting on the scapulars and covert tips. The large facial disc is plain brown with a narrow blackish rim, and the large eyes are black. It occurs in both grey and rufous phases, the latter being the commonest in Britain. More often heard than seen, it hides well during the daytime yet its roost may be betrayed by noisy mobbing Blackbirds and other songbirds, or spotted by diligent observers searching likely trees. On drizzly evenings it may emerge from the roost before darkness. Essentially a woodland bird, but it can

FLEDGLING

be found wherever large old oaks and other mature broad-leaved trees occur, such as in parks, gardens, churchyards and wooded farmland, as well as in mixed woodland and mature coniferous forest. It is the most familiar and widespread owl in our region, even penetrating urban areas if habitat is available, and is therefore the most likely owl to be encountered in a garden.

ADULT

The nest is typically in a hollow tree, in a cavity with a large enough opening, but also more rarely in buildings or in an old crow's nest or similar. They will use nest boxes and can therefore be attracted to nest in a large garden, favouring a big box with a large entrance and a deep interior. No nest material is used, and breeding commences in March with the female incubating two or three eggs for 30 days. For the first three weeks after hatching, the female broods the chicks while the male hunts and brings food. After this period the female also hunts and the young fledge after 35–39 days.

The familiar song or advertising call is a series of hollow-sounding hooting notes, erroneously described by the wider non-birding general public (with a helping hand from William Shakespeare!) as "too'whit-too'woo". Sung by the male at dusk and during the night, the initial note is a strong hoot, followed by a pause of two to four seconds, then a short introductory hoot swiftly followed by a shivering sequence of rapid 'hoo-ing', with a longer final hoot being

in comparable in strength to the first, as in "hoooooo.......hu'- hu'hu'hu'hu' hoooooh!" or "hwaooow.......hw'- hwa'ow'ow'- oooow". The female sometimes gives a shorter simpler hooting in a similar pattern, and both sexes give a loud, sharp contact call, "ke'vick" or "ae'wick", rising quite sharply on the second note and sometimes heard in response to the hooting call. A variant of this is sometimes repeated sharply in alarm, as in "kvik kvik kvik". A rarely heard bubbling trill is also given by both sexes during courtship, but is only audible at close range. Juvenile birds make a "psee'hip" call.

Swift
Apus apus

Length: 16–17cm
Wingspan: 42–48cm

A remarkably well-adapted bird, leading an almost entirely aerial life. A true harbinger of summer, its arrival in the sky is a welcome and uplifting sign that warmer weather is on its way. It is remarkably regular in its arrival every year, always to within a few days, and it is a sad day when the flocks depart again (typically in mid-August, but with regional variations). Often confused with Swallows and House Martins by novices, the plumage, flight action, shape and voice of the Swift are all pointers for easy separation.

The plumage is uniformly dark brown, although often appearing black at range or in poor light, and with a whitish throat. It has a slender cigar-like body with a short forked tail, a short rounded head and very long and narrow sickle-shaped wings that are almost entirely 'hand', the 'elbow' or carpal joint lying very close to the body. Swifts have very small feet that are only designed for clinging to rock faces, and they never perch except to roost and when visiting the nest. They fly strongly, their narrow wings appearing to flicker in rapid flight, although for most of the time they glide or soar, even sleeping on the wing, which they achieve through shutting down one hemisphere of the brain at a time.

Swifts are found over virtually every habitat, the choice dictated only by the availability of flying insects. They can often be seen feeding low over water bodies in poor weather, conditions under which aquatic insects are more likely to emerge than terrestrial ones. They avoid large weather systems, leaving the area completely, but in fine weather use all available airspace and are a regular summer sight over most gardens.

Originally adapted to nesting in cliff crevices or even in cavities in trees, in modern times Swifts have nested in urban areas, in older buildings,

churches and houses, using roof eaves, spaces under dislodged tiles, wall cavities and any available crack or crevice. They have suffered in recent years from modern building techniques that exclude them from such nesting sites. The nest is made of windblown plant material that is collected in the air, and then glued together with saliva to make a shallow cup. Two or three eggs are laid from the end of May and are incubated for 18–20 days by both adults, although the eggs are adapted to withstand cooling and incubation periods can be longer. The young are fed by both parents, who bring a mass of insects packed into their visibly bulging throats. The chicks remain in the nest for 35–56 days and can withstand periods of hunger during bad weather by living off their fat reserves, although this extends the time spent inside the nest. They are fully independent once they fly the nest. Swifts can be lured to a nest site or a commercially available swift nest box by the playing of recordings

(which can be purchased on CD or downloaded free at www. commonswift.org) specially designed to attract them. They are sociable creatures and appear to thrive on nesting colonially; recordings can be played in the first weeks after their arrival from Africa, as well as later in the breeding season, when the previous year's young are prospecting for next year's nest sites.

During the breeding season Swifts are quite vocal, particularly in the evening, when nesting birds will perform a group screaming display, racing around their loose colony in a fast-moving flock, sometimes joined by other birds calling from within their nests. Non-breeders will also do this when gathering prior to ascending to higher altitudes for aerial roosting. The calls are high-pitched, shrill trilling sounds, varying in pitch and tempo, as in "rrrheeeiiii….", "ssrrriiii..", "zrrreeee.." or "iiiiirrrrrreeeeeee..", sometimes begun more slowly with hoarse stuttering sounds.

Kingfisher
Alcedo atthis

Length: 16–17cm
Wingspan: 24–26cm

The Kingfisher is unique among our birds in its brilliant and dazzling plumage, and it is an unusual yet by no means exceptional visitor to gardens. It is beautifully coloured, with a bright, pale blue back and uppertail that catch the attention, particularly when in flight, and a darker turquoise

MALE

PLUNGING
FOR FISH

blue on the crown, nape, wings and scapulars, which can appear greenish in certain lights. The underparts and cheeks are rufous-orange, the throat is white, with a white patch also on the neck to the rear of the cheek. Apart from its coloration, it also has a distinctive shape, being a small, dumpy bird with a short tail, short legs, large head and a long powerful bill. It sits motionless while searching for fish, usually on a branch or post in a discreet and undisturbed section of a river or lakeside corner, and plunges suddenly to catch prey. It is most frequently seen in fast direct flight low over the surface of the water, attention being drawn by its distinct call as it shoots past.

Typically found in freshwater habitats, favouring a slow, fish-rich river or stream, the Kingfisher can also be found on canals, lakes, reservoirs, dykes, ditches and fishponds. Outside the breeding season it can sometimes be found in marine habitats such as lagoons, sheltered rocky coasts and estuaries. It may be seen in a garden in a suburban or rural environment, but this is almost totally dependent on the availability within the garden of a water feature such as a stream or large pond containing small fish, as well as the presence of a suitable fishing perch. In spring they have an eye-catching display with aerial chases and bowing and stretching displays on the ground, fanning their wings out to show off the colour of the back and rump.

Both sexes help excavate a long, slightly upwards-sloping nest burrow in a suitably soft earth bank by a slow-flowing river, with some trees or bushy margins to provide cover and fishing perches. The burrow is usually some 60–100cm above the water and 40–120cm deep, with a circular interior chamber of approximately 15cm in diameter. Five to seven eggs are laid and

are incubated by both sexes for 20–21 days, the young being fed by both parents. They fledge after 23–26 days, and there are occasionally two broods.

As is so often the case with brightly coloured birds, Kingfisher calls are simple and uncomplicated. The most commonly heard is a sharp, high-pitched and penetrating whistle, a "tszeeee!", or "peeeep", extended into a repeated disyllabic "ti-peeee ti-peeee ti-peeee" or "zii!'eeeee! zii!'eeeee!", often given in flight and frequently the first or only indication of the presence of the species as it zips past in a high-speed blur of blue. It also gives a softer and more conversational "pee-pee-pee". In spring it is occasionally heard to give a sweet and varied song of trilling whistles and sometimes a rich warble, and pairs will engage in noisy chases during courtship.

FEMALE

Green Woodpecker
Picus viridis

Length: 31–33cm
Wingspan: 40–42cm

MALE

The second-largest woodpecker in Europe (after the mighty Black, not described here) and a brightly coloured bird with green upperparts and a fairly well-contrasting yellow-green rump, which is particularly noticeable in flight. The underparts are pale greenish-grey, and it has a long and powerful horn-coloured bill. The head and face are boldly marked, with a red crown that extends to the nape and a black face punctuated with a staring white eye. It has a short black moustache that is centred with red in the male but is all black in the female. The flight of all woodpeckers is very characteristic; as the tail is short and stiff, it cannot be used as a rudder when the bird is flying and the flight pattern therefore takes the form of deeply undulating bounds, with the wings held close in to the body every three or four wingbeats. Green Woodpeckers spend more time on the ground than any other woodpecker, with a distinctive and fairly upright carriage and the tail held low. Turf-dwelling ants are

JUVENILE

FEMALE

a favourite food, and it has a very long tongue with which to lick them up.

A familiar and common bird that is resident across our region. It avoids dense forest and is found in open broad-leaved woodlands with clearings, forest edge, large gardens, parkland, orchards, hedges with mature trees, farmland, rough grassland and heaths with scattered trees. It can often be encountered on the ground in areas with open ground, and especially on grassy areas such as lawns, golf courses and pastures. Green Woodpeckers are most likely to be encountered in larger suburban and rural gardens with mature deciduous trees and a lawn or grassy area for feeding. They are quite vocal, and can be heard particularly in the early morning, and also before and after rain. The nest hole is excavated by both sexes, in a mature tree with a fairly large circular or oval entrance hole leading to an unlined cavity that is 30–60cm deep. Nesting commences in April or May, when four to six eggs are laid and incubated by both

sexes for 19–20 days. After hatching, both parents feed the chicks a semi-liquid regurgitated mass, with fledging taking place after 21–24 days. Green Woodpeckers will occasionally use nest boxes.

The advertising call of the male, usually sung from high up in a large tree, is a far-carrying, slightly accelerating, laughing series of notes "hwa'hwa'hwa'hwa'hwa'hwa....", colloquially described as a 'yaffling'. It typically lasts for 1–3 seconds, dropping in pitch towards the end of the call and with a rate of about six 'yaffs' per second. The female gives a shorter, flatter 'yaffle', not dissimilar to the call of the Whimbrel. In flight both sexes give a loud, chuckling and often-repeated call of three or four syllables, as in "chyuk'chyuk'chyuk'chyuk" or "kye'kye'kye", also expressed when perched as an alarm or excitement call, and frequently given by young birds that are still accompanying their parents. The drum is rarely heard, but is said to be fairly quiet and 1.5 seconds in duration.

Great Spotted Woodpecker

Dendrocopos major

Length: 22–23cm
Wingspan: 34–39cm

A familiar bird across most of our region, and perhaps the most likely woodpecker to be encountered in a garden. The upperparts are black patterned with white, with two large oval white patches on the scapulars being the boldest plumage feature. The flight feathers are banded with white transverse bars, and

MALE

JUVENILE
AT FEEDER

the short stiff tail is black, with white outer tail feathers barred with black. It has a black nape and crown, with a large white cheek patch enclosed by a black 'bridle', which loops from the bill to the rear of the cheek, plus a smaller white patch set within the black on the sides of the neck. The undertail coverts are crimson, and the remaining underparts are buffish-white. In the male, there is a distinct patch of red on the nape, lacking in the female. Juvenile birds have red crowns, a readily visible feature on well-grown chicks when peeking out of their nest hole, but a potentially confusing aspect when a youngster is seen on its own away from the nest.

A resident, and the commonest of its family in northern and western Europe, it is found in all types of forest, both deciduous and coniferous, as well as in mature hedges, large gardens, parkland and smaller wooded patches. More northerly populations may disperse southwards when cone crops fail, and migrants can appear in coastal habitats and even on treeless islands. 'Great-spots' roam quite widely, and regularly visit garden peanut feeders and fat balls, or forage in the more natural parts of a garden. They are also quite notorious for their dark side – they will rob other birds' nests of young chicks, even enlarging the holes of tit boxes to gain access to the young inside.

The nest is a hole bored by both sexes in a suitable tree, with a tunnel leading to a rounded cavity about 30cm deep. Breeding commences in May, and four to six eggs are laid and incubated mainly, but not exclusively, by the female. The chicks hatch after 14–16 days and fledge after a further 20–24 days. It is often easy to find nests with well-grown youngsters, as they draw attention to themselves by poking their heads out of the hole and noisily and continuously begging for food.

Attention is usually drawn by its call, as it shins up a tree trunk or flies in strongly undulating flight from one patch of trees to the next, uttering a loud "pick!"' or "kik". Usually uttered singly, a series of rapidly repeated excited calls, at a rate of three per second, is given when a threat is perceived near the nest, accelerating into a hard rattling trill on occasions. It also has a softer "tchick". When the young in the nest are near fledging, they give a persistent, fairly high-pitched begging call, of a rapidly repeated short trill of four notes reminiscent of one of the calls of the Kestrel. In spring the drumming can be heard frequently, a resonant mechanical raining of

FEMALE
FEEDING

blows on a suitably dry branch, often at the very top of a tree. The drum typically lasts for between 0.5 and 0.7 of a second, and includes 12–14 'knocks'. The drumming is done by both sexes, usually between February and May, with the females drumming in the earlier part of this period.

Lesser Spotted Woodpecker

Dendrocopos minor

Length: 14–15cm

Wingspan: 25–27cm

Much the smallest of our woodpeckers, and at 17–25g just 25 per cent of the weight of the Great Spotted Woodpecker, its closest relative in Britain and northern Europe. It has a short stubby bill in comparison to other woodpeckers, and a small rounded head. The underparts are whitish, with no red on the vent, and a prominent black submoustachial stripe runs from the bill, flaring on the side of the neck before dispersing downwards into small fine streaks on the flanks. The upperparts are black, cross-barred with white bands from mantle to flight feathers, giving a 'ladder-back' effect. The male has a red crown outlined in black, while the female has a completely black crown, with a small buffy-white patch restricted to the forehead. A rather unobtrusive bird, most often seen in late winter and early spring before the trees come into leaf, and when their calls and drumming draw attention.

Resident in our region, although due to its small size and rather secretive nature it is easily overlooked. It has undergone a rapid decline in Britain since 1980, and has disappeared from many former haunts. It can be found in broad-leaved and mixed woodlands, favouring parks, large gardens, orchards, copses, groves and alder trees along river valleys, but ranging into more marginal habitats during winter. An exciting yet quite possible visitor to gardens containing or adjoining suitable habitat, it feeds on insects by gleaning along trunks, small branches and twigs, and requires a good supply of decaying wood. It is also known to 'flycatch', sallying forth from small branches.

MALE

FEMALE

Breeding commences in April and May, and the nest is a hole bored by both adults, often in a side branch and with an entrance hole of about 30mm wide, from which a tunnel leads to an elongated chamber. They will also occasionally use nest boxes, requiring a standard box with an entrance hole of 50mm. Four to six eggs are laid and incubated for 14–15 days by both sexes. Both adults feed the young, which fledge after 19–22 days.

The short "chick" call is similar to and confusable with that of the Great Spotted, yet is weaker, higher pitched and less far-carrying. The advertising call is a long, fast series of rather shrill piping notes: "e-pee'pee'pee'peee'pee'pee 'pee" or "qwi'qwi'qwi'qwi'qwi…", sometimes trailing away at the end. It is rather similar to the calls of the Wryneck and Kestrel and, although primarily used in the breeding season, it may be heard at other times, as is the drumming, used as a territorial 'call'. The Lesser Spotted Woodpecker drums faster, longer and more evenly than the Great, lacking the 'drum roll' and lasting up to 1.75 seconds at a rate of 18–19 'hits' per second.

Skylark
Alauda arvensis

Length: 17–18cm
Wingspan: 30–36cm

A familiar bird of arable country and open grassy spaces, the Skylark is of course best known for its glorious song, typically (but not exclusively) given in a hovering song flight. A rather robust bird, with a stubby half-crest and broad wings with a distinct whitish trailing edge. It has white outer tail feathers and a distinctively hesitant and fluttering flight action, with much hovering and dithering in the air. The plumage is unspectacular, the upperparts streaked blackish on buffy-brown and the crown is finely streaked black. The face is pale with a whitish supercilium, lores and eye-ring, and the underparts are whitish with clear blackish streaking on the upper breast forming an obvious breast band.

A bird of open country and farmland, the Skylark is frequently found in and around cultivated fields and also favours grasslands, coastal meadows, golf courses, dunes, pastures, heaths, heather moors and grassy hilltops. It requires open, flat areas and occurs in low stature crops and herbage, as well as in taller crops, so long as open ground is available nearby. Modern farming methods – especially the autumn sowing of cereal crops – have had a dramatic impact on Skylark populations, which have declined greatly since the 1970s. This is due to the reduced number of stubble fields in winter, and also to crops growing too tall too early, which prevents later breeding attempts. Open blocks of ground within autumn-sown crops, known as 'Skylark plots', can provide a simple and effective solution. Western European birds are generally resident, and supplemented in winter by migrant birds from further north and east, which can form large flocks. Migrating birds are easily located by call as they pass overhead, and this is the method by which most garden-related Skylark records are made, although gardens with large open grassy areas adjacent to open country can attract Skylarks in their own right.

Breeding commences in April, with up to four broods per pair in a good year. Three or four eggs are laid in a shallow cup in a depression on the ground, lined with grasses. The female incubates for 13–14 days, and both parents feed the hatched young. The young leave the nest after 9–10 days and are able to fly after 20 days.

The song is a familiar sound, a melodious collection of sweet chirruping and whistling phrases with a hypnotic cyclical quality. Typically it is sung without a break for up to five minutes,

occasionally for longer, and usually commencing from take-off as the bird ascends into its song flight, which takes it high into the sky. It sometimes includes mimicry of other species, and will sing freely from the ground, although in a less exuberant version. The calls are frequently heard, a variable but bright-sounding dry rolling chirrup, such as "prrr'id", "churrrrip", "prrr'i'i'ew", "pruurt", "pree'eep", "rreep'chechew", often sounding rather slurred. When given in flight, it is these calls that will draw the attention of the observer to migrating birds, which can occur over any habitat.

Swallow
Hirundo rustica

Length: 17–19cm (inc. tail streamers of up to 6.5cm)
Wingspan: 32–34.5cm

The classic harbinger of spring, when this elegant and streamlined bird arrives in Europe from its winter quarters in Africa. Very aerial, with a light and graceful flight punctuated with rapid swoops after insects, it has a deeply forked tail with narrow elongated streamers on the outer tail feathers and which, when spread, shows white spots on the feather webs. The upperparts are a glossy midnight-blue, with a deep red forehead and throat, a dark blue breast band and buffish-cream underparts. Immature birds have short tail streamers and a dingy buff throat. Swallows perch freely on wires and buildings, although rarely on the ground except when gathering nesting material. Although less gregarious than their close relatives, they can form large flocks prior to their southward autumn migration. Whilst migrating they typically fly in a straight line, in a determined fashion and often close to the ground.

As an aerial feeder dependent on flying insects, it can exploit a very wide range of habitats provided that food is plentiful. Although tending to avoid densely forested and mountainous areas, it otherwise occurs in all types of open country, but most commonly in farmland and villages where grazing animals are present. It can be seen feeding low over meadows and pastures and also over freshwater bodies, marshes and other wetlands. It is also dependent on suitable nesting places, favouring partly open farm buildings, barns, outhouses, stables and other man-made structures. Being so aerial Swallows can be recorded over many gardens, either as migrants passing overhead or simply feeding in the area if the garden is adjacent to suitable breeding and feeding habitat. They can be regular garden visitors in more rural environments, with nesting occurring within a garden if the right conditions are available.

SWALLOWS AND
HOUSE MARTINS

incubates for 14–16 days, after which both sexes feed the young until fledging occurs in 17–24 days. The young continue to roost in the nest for the first few days. There are usually two broods and sometimes three.

The song is a melodious twittering and spluttering, periodically interspersed with a strangled croak followed by a trilling rattle, and can be sung persistently, either in flight or from a perch such as a wire. Sub-song or short twittering phrases are frequently heard, as in "wttwtitwttwwtit". It has a variety of calls, such as a commonly heard "vhit!", often repeated as "vhit vhit vhit", and a sharp, higher-pitched, slightly ascending "vheet! vheet!" or "plee-vhink", uttered as an alarm call in response to aerial predators. Other variations of calls are a conversational "tit'tich'iwitt" and "wtwittit", a quick "thwitt" and a sharp "tjjup!".

The nest is an open shallow cup-shaped structure stuck on to a vertical surface with the support of a ledge or rafter, and is built by both adults. It is made of mud pellets mixed with fine plant fibres and lined with feathers. Breeding begins in May, and four or five eggs are laid. The female

House Martin
Delichon urbica

Length: 13–15cm
Wingspan: 26–29cm

A familiar bird in suburban areas and villages, this is a dumpy and compact swallow with a simple and seemingly monochrome plumage pattern. It has blue-black upperparts, cap and tail, with a large white rump that serves as its most distinctive plumage character, easily seen in any view except for when the bird is directly overhead. The underside of the body and the underwing coverts are white, and the feet are feathered white, a visible feature when the bird is perched. The tail is rather short, but shows a prominent fork. The flight action is rather different to that of other swallows in our region, being slower with much gliding on straight wings, often in long lazy arcs, and it often flies high up when feeding. It perches freely on wires and on buildings, as well as on the ground when collecting mud for its nest. It is fairly sociable and gregarious, and large groups can be seen gathering on wires, especially after the young have fledged.

A summer visitor from Africa, typically present in northern Europe between April and October. Originally a cliff-nester, which is still the case in some parts of its range, it is now more commonly found around towns and villages. It avoids densely forested areas, and is less tied to water than some of its relatives. House Martins are frequently seen around gardens, owing to their choice of nesting

usually reflect the availability of a nearby source. The nest is made of mud pellets strengthened with plant fibres and lined with feathers, and takes both adults about 10 days to build. The nest is a deep and rounded half-cup, adhered to a vertical surface and with a small entrance at the top. Each nest contains roughly 1000 pellets of mud. Breeding occurs from May onwards, and four or five eggs are laid and incubated by both sexes for 13–19 days. The young are fed by both sexes and fledge after 19–25 days.

The commonly heard note is the contact call, a short dry stony rattle with a bright quality, as in "prrrt", either monosyllabic or often repeated two or three times in rapid succession, such as "jijitt", "prrrr-tit" and "jrrrr-tit'it". It also gives a shrill descending "schreeeo" as an anxiety call, often in response to aerial predators. All of these calls are typically heard from flying birds. The song is a made up of several call notes run together, plus a throaty rapid warbling, without any structured phrases, a rambling chuntering that is sung usually when close to the breeding area or at the nest itself.

habitat, and can be attracted to artificial nest boxes placed under the eaves of a house. They are easily seen over urban areas, hawking for insects high in the sky and often in the company of Swifts.

The nest is a closed mud-built structure, typically located under the eaves of houses but also on bridges and other man-made structures, and as a consequence it can be quite confiding of humans. Several nests are often built close together in a small colony, and it requires a good supply of mud with which to build its nest, so breeding sites will

Meadow Pipit
Anthus pratensis

Length: 14.5–15.5cm

Wingspan: 22–25cm

This is perhaps the archetypal 'little brown bird', with few features to distinguish it! It is olive-brown on the upperparts, well streaked with black on the mantle, plain on the rump, with bold white outer tail feathers. The brown crown is streaked black, the bill is slender with a mostly yellowish lower mandible, and the face is pale with pale lores and a short diffuse pale eyebrow. The underparts are whitish to pale buff, with a bold malar stripe, clear black spots and streaks on the breast extending down onto the flanks. The legs are pinkish. It is quite an active and lively little bird, often very noticeable as it flies around calling.

It favours open country, breeding in grassland, meadows, coastal pastures, saltmarshes, heaths, young plantations and moorland, where it can often be abundant. Birds that breed at higher elevations descend in winter, and populations in temperate western Europe are usually resident, their numbers supplemented

MEADOW PIPIT (FRONT)
AND LINNETS

in winter by birds arriving from areas further north and east, where they tend to be migratory. Outside the breeding season they range more widely, into virtually any open country such as farmland, wetlands, beaches, golf courses and playing fields, and it is at this time that they are most likely to be recorded from gardens, attention being drawn to the thin little calls as migrants pass low overhead. Where a garden is adjacent to suitable grassy and open habitats, birds may appear on the ground, walking (not hopping) and feeding on a lawn, or in more rural areas during the breeding season they might be audible as they perform their song flights nearby.

Nesting occurs from April, and four or five eggs are laid in a cup-shaped nest on the ground, often invisible from above and tucked into the base of a grassy tussock. The incubation is done by the female and lasts 13–15 days, and upon hatching the young are fed by both parents. Fledging occurs after 12–14 days, and there are usually two broods per year.

The commonly heard call, frequently uttered on take-off, is a thin "tssit'ssit'ssit", typically repeated in triplets although also often singly, sometimes with a variation, as in "weesp". A more abbreviated "ssit" or "chip" note is also given, and the anxiety call – used frequently near the nest – is a rapid clipped "tse'tut". The song is bright and bubbling, rapidly accelerating with much variety in tone and with rattling trills thrown in, such as "tsilp tsilp tsilp tsilp'tsilp'tsilp'tsilp'tttrrrrrrrr bl'bl'bl'bl 'bl'bli'bli'bli'bli", and often with a few buoyant "bing bing bing" notes added. The pitch and harshness vary between songsters. The full song is only delivered in a parachuting display flight, but birds frequently sing from the ground with a shorter simpler version of repeated introductory notes.

Grey Wagtail
Motacilla cinerea

Length: 17–20cm
Wingspan: 25–27cm

An elegant and attractive bird, the Grey Wagtail is characterized by its very long white-edged tail, which is pumped continuously, rocking the whole rear end of the bird. Although its choice of habitat is often a clue to its identity, in all plumages it shows a bright yellow vent and brownish-pink legs. The head and mantle are pure grey, and the wings are blackish with white edges to the long tertial feathers. In summer the male is rich yellow on the breast, with a bright white supercilium and submoustachial stripes framing a solid black throat. The female typically has a white or dingy greyish throat, a buff supercilium and paler yellow underparts. In winter both sexes show a white throat, with pale whitish-yellow underparts. Young birds are similar to females, but are more buff-coloured on the underparts, with whitish wingbars and a greener-tinged rump.

More closely tied to water than its relatives, it frequents fast-flowing streams and rivers, canals, lakesides and some larger, slower rivers, so long as there are perches on rocks, shingle, weirs and locks, and cavities for nests in walls, roofs, rocks and culverts. It is commonly found on upland and mountain streams, and outside

WINTER PLUMAGE

MALE SUMMER
PLUMAGE

the breeding season ranges more widely into lowland areas, also occurring on estuaries, coasts and sewage farms. It also turns up in towns and cities, often using the flat roofs of tall buildings where rainwater collects. It can readily occur in gardens, particularly if water features are present, but in most inhabited areas it will appear only outside the breeding season. The distinctive flight call makes it noticeable, and may be heard from gardens in urban areas as birds fly between choice rooftop habitats.

Nesting commences in April, and the nest is a solid mass of twigs, moss, leaves and grass built by the female, often hidden from view behind some vegetation. Five eggs are laid and incubated mostly by the female for about 13 days, and the chicks are fed by both parents. They fledge after 14–15 days.

The vocalizations are high pitched and rather penetrating, as is usual for birds living by rivers, which produce a lot of low-frequency noise. The typical call is a disyllabic "dji'dih" or "chiddih", also uttered singly as "djitd" and often heard in flight. The anxiety call when near the nest is a rising "sweee" or "chwea". There is also a three- or four-syllable penetrating high-pitched call "tsi'tsi'tsi'tsi". The song is a bright, high-pitched tinkling series of varying phrases of notes, such as "di di ti'ti'ti chichichi chew trrrrrrr pink pink pink see-chew". Another phrase sometimes introduced or sung singly is a simple "si'si'si see-chew".

Pied Wagtail & White Wagtail
Motacilla alba

Length: 16.5–19cm

Wingspan: 25–30cm

Two forms of the same species occur in our region, the Pied Wagtail *M. alba yarrelli*, found in Britain and along the Continental Channel coast, and the White Wagtail *M. alba alba*, which occurs across mainland Europe. This is an unmistakable bird, with its long wagging tail and striking black-and-white plumage, and it has a bounding and undulating flight. In the Pied Wagtail, the back is jet black on the male, dark grey in the female, with little or no contrast between the back and black nape. Both sexes have a blackish rump and boldly patterned wings with white feather edgings to black feathers. The face and cheeks are white, and in summer it has a bold black throat and breast, most extensive in the male. The White Wagtail differs in having an ash-grey mantle that contrasts sharply with its black cap and nape, a feature that is less well defined in the female. In winter both forms acquire a white throat, the black being reduced to a broad crescent across the breast. Juveniles are similar to winter females but have a buffy wash on the face and breast and are browner above.

In western Europe birds are semi-resident, while elsewhere they are summer visitors. Found in a wide range of open habitats, typically close to wet areas such as lakes, rivers, streams, gravel pits, estuaries and coasts, they favour open areas such as farmland, fields, pastures, parks, gardens, airfields, golf courses and along roads, ideally where water is present, but most importantly where there are flat open areas in which to seek food. It is also regularly found in towns and villages, around buildings with suitable adjacent habitat. It often forms communal roosts in

MALE PIED WAGTAIL (*M. A. YARRELLI*)
SUMMER PLUMAGE

MALE WHITE WAGTAIL
(*M. A. ALBA*) SUMMER PLUMAGE

creepers or ferns, although open-fronted nest boxes are also used. The female builds a solid mass of twigs, moss, grass and leaves, lined with feathers, wool and hair, and lays five or six eggs. These are incubated by the female for 12–14 days, and the young are tended by both parents. They fledge the nest after 14–15 days.

The commonly heard calls are an emphatic high-pitched disyllabic "chissick", sometimes uttered as a single syllable "chitt" or "tschick", and the flight call, which is a thinner-sounding and more liquid "tsli-wee", "tslee-vit" or a trisyllabic "tslee-li-vit". Another call is a more slurred and slightly descending "tzwerr'p". The song, given at a fast tempo when in a state of excitement, such as in display or alarm, is a very rapid sequence of call notes run together in varying pitches, with harder single-syllable notes dominating the structure and interspersed with higher liquid notes. It also gives a more languid song, a series of twittering notes interspersed with pauses.

urban areas in winter, on large city buildings such as office blocks, hospitals and supermarkets, the birds packing in on window ledges, rooftops or in adjacent trees. The Pied Wagtail is very widespread across Britain and can occur in gardens almost anywhere.

The nest is typically in a cavity in a wall, roof, building, pipe or similar, often hidden behind

FEMALE
PIED

Waxwing
Bombycilla garrulus

Length: 18–21cm
Wingspan: 32–35cm

The Waxwing is perhaps one of the most exotic-looking and exciting visitors likely to be encountered in a garden. Roughly the size of a Starling, this gorgeous bird is rather plumper, thicker-necked and more compact. The plumage overall is a pinky grey-brown, with a greyer rump, a striking chestnut vent and a band of yellow on the tail-tip that is broadest on the male. The head is distinctively patterned with a prominent soft crest, a black throat and loral patch that extends behind the eye, a white spot at the bill base and a richer chestnut tone on the cheek and forehead. The wings of the male are boldly patterned with white bands on the primary coverts and secondary tips, the latter having little red waxy appendages which give the bird its name. The primaries have sharp white crescents on the very tips and yellow tips on the outer webs, forming a bold yellow line on the closed wing. These features are duller and somewhat reduced on females, and lacking altogether in young birds, which also have the black on the throat restricted to the chin.

A winter visitor to Britain, irruptive and irregular in its occurrence. In some years there are large invasions across the country, and in other years very few are recorded. Typically gathering in flocks, they can be found wherever their favourite winter diet food of berries is available, and have a particular liking for Rowan and other

Sorbus species. They also favour many types of introduced berry-bearing trees and bushes, and as a consequence can appear in roadside trees, hedgerows, parks and gardens, and frequently in the grounds of supermarkets, hospitals and other recently landscaped areas, where ornamental bushes provide a ready source of food for this delightful visitor from the Arctic. They can be attracted to gardens with suitable berry bushes, but will also eat fruit put out for them, especially apples. Often the first indication of Waxwings in an area is their call, as they fly over or gather on wires and rooftop aerials.

In summer they breed in boreal mature coniferous forest rich in lichen, feeding on insects and often engaging in flycatching sallies from the tops of tall trees, and are unusual in that they neither hold breeding territories nor defend a feeding territory. The nest is built from twigs, moss and lichen, typically in a pine or spruce.

The call of the Waxwing is a distinctive silvery trilling "srrrrrrrrr", often given in half-second bursts although often for longer, at a rate of about 22 notes per second. As they are most frequently encountered in our region in winter flocks, this trilling can be continuous when many birds are calling, and is given most emphatically just prior to flight. The song is never heard in Britain, and only rarely on the breeding grounds – possibly little used there due to the lack of territoriality on the breeding grounds. It is a slow and halting combination of trilling phrases and harsh raucous sounds, as in "srrrrrr sirrrrrr chark chark chi-chark srrrrrrr srrrrrrr" etc.

Wren
Troglodytes troglodytes

Length: 9–10cm

Wingspan: 13–17cm

The Wren is one of the most abundant birds in
Europe, with an estimated eight million territories
in Britain alone, where it is resident throughout
and found in a wide range of habitats. A tiny
and restless little brown bird, with the distinctive
habit of cocking its tail up and over its back, it is
rather furtive and heard more often than it is seen.
Frequently found skulking in dense undergrowth,
it usually forages near to the ground and can be
seen disappearing into crevices as it searches
for invertebrates or flying between cover like a
brown bee. The upperparts and head are a warm

reddish-brown, and the short wings are finely vermiculated and barred. The underparts are paler with mottling on the flanks. It has a slender bill and a distinctive long pale creamy supercilium.

A widespread and common bird throughout our region, particularly in woodland with dense undergrowth, also in scrub, hedges, gardens, parks, moorland where bracken-filled gullies offer shelter, sea cliffs and other rocky places with crevices, and occurring up to the treeline in some parts of its range. It is one of our more familiar garden birds, often nesting in a garden in almost any type of hole or cavity, even in unusual places in sheds, garages and other artificial structures. They roost communally in winter, cramming themselves into a nest or cavity, with their tails pointing outwards. The highest number of Wrens recorded at one such roost is an incredible 96!

Breeding commences in April, and the male Wren makes several nests of leaves, moss and grass; from these the female will select one that is to her liking and then line it with feathers. She will lay five or six eggs and incubate them alone for 16–18 days. Both parents feed the young, which fledge after 15–18 days. Although the species is single-brooded, the males are polygamous, sometimes having more than one female and accompanying nest at any one time, and staggering the timing so that they can help feed the young of each brood. Wrens easily desert their nest in the early stages of breeding, and care should therefore be taken not to disturb them.

Very vocal, with typical call notes being a hard "tchek" or "chudt", often extended into "tchek'eck'eck".   It also gives a low rattling churr. When anxious, near the nest or young, or in response to danger such as a cat, it gives a higher-pitched hard rattle, not unlike someone sucking on the corner of their mouth to produce a rasping sound, as in "tr'tr'tr'tr'tr'tr'tr". The song is remarkably loud and shrill for such a tiny bird, and is a very rapid series of well-structured piercing notes, usually including or ending with a loud trill. It usually lasts for 4–7 seconds, during which time it produces about 6–8 notes per second, such as "see'se'seow'see'seee'ch'ch'ch'ch'ch'see'suwi's uwi'see'su'ee'trrrrrrrrrr chu'chu'see!".

Dunnock
Prunella modularis

Length: 13–14.5cm
Wingspan: 19–21cm

A demure little bird that is frequently seen in gardens, although often skulking and unobtrusive, and usually seen shuffling, mouse-like, on the ground. Brown and grey, with a warm brown mantle clearly streaked with black, and dull grey-brown underparts with mottled brown streaks along the flanks. The head, neck, throat and breast are a clean lead-grey, with brown cheeks and a darker mottled crown. The bill is thin, black and warbler-like, and the legs are orange. Juveniles are plain brown, streaked and blotched with black, and with a whitish throat.

A familiar resident garden bird in Britain, and found anywhere with dense scrubby undergrowth. It is commonly encountered in gardens, parks, churchyards, open mixed woodland, farms, scrub, hedges, young conifer plantations, heaths and overgrown rough ground in urban areas, such as railway embankments, especially where it is a

DISPLAYING MALE

JUVENILE

little damp. It is attached to spruce forest in the northern parts of its range, where it is usually just a summer visitor. Primarily insectivorous, it does not use seed or nut feeders but in winter will eat small pieces of nut, seed kernels or nyger seed, taken from the ground.

Despite being something of a 'boring brown bird', it has rather exotic and complex breeding arrangements. Dunnocks are polyandrous, meaning that the female has two males in attendance, although this can extend to three females and three males, all in overlapping relationships! A typical scenario is where two males will sing and defend a territory for a single female, with both males courting her for sexual favours. The display of the male involves an eye-catching alternate wing-flicking, which serves to attract a female. A male intent on mating may be seen to peck around the cloaca of the female, to trigger an expulsion of sperm from another male that she has recently mated with. DNA studies of chicks have found that within a single brood there may be two fathers contributing. The nest is a stout cup of twigs and moss, lined with hair, wool or fine moss and built within a dense bush or hedge. Breeding commences in April, with four or five eggs being laid and incubated by the female for 14–15 days. The young are fed by both (or all!) parents, fledging after 12–15 days. There are two and sometimes three, broods.

The common call is a rather coarse, high-pitched "tiih", often repeated a number of times and made as both a contact call and as an alarm. It also utters a thinner, less coarse "seep", and a shivering "ititititi", which is typically given outside the breeding season and is rather like the alarm call but more silvery in quality. The song is a high-pitched and scratchy little ditty, fairly rapid and expressed on a level tone without trills or flourishes, confusable with the song of the Wren but slower and much less emphatic, lasting between 1.5–3 seconds but also delivered in longer phrases. It is rather regular and unvarying, as in "ss'tsi'ti'si'ti'teew'ti'ti'deuw'tii'si'si'ti".

Robin
Erithacus rubecula

Length: 12.5–14cm
Wingspan: 20–22cm

A familiar garden bird for many, this is a delicate but plump bird, with brown upperparts and crown, a narrow buff wingbar, and a large orange-red breast extending across the face and over the bill, rimmed with a blue-grey border. The underparts are whitish with a brown wash on the flanks. Juvenile birds have the familiar rotund shape but are brown above with buff spotting, while the underparts are buff with dark spotting on the breast. They assume the adult-type plumage fairly quickly, gradually acquiring the patches of tangerine on the breast. Ground feeders, Robins hop along and pause watchfully, with flicks of the wings and tail. They are famously aggressive towards other Robins that stray within their territory, sometimes attacking the intruder in such a frenzy that it is blinded or even killed.

Essentially a forest bird, found in shady woodland with undergrowth, it is also commonly seen in gardens, parks and other managed places offering dense cover. In Britain it is a widespread resident and notably confiding, although in northern Europe it is migratory, frequents coniferous forest, and is much more retiring. The Robin is one of the most familiar British garden birds, notably tame when any digging is going on in the garden. It will perch nearby to take worms or other invertebrates unearthed by the gardener, a variation of natural behaviour in which it might follow Wild Boar in close attendance as they churn up the ground. Robins will visit feeders and bird

tables, and have a special liking for live food such as mealworms. As terrestrial feeders, they are very vulnerable to domestic cats. It has been estimated that cats kill 15 Robins for every one killed by natural predators such as Sparrowhawks.

Robins choose a wide variety of sites for nest-building, with any form of depression or hole considered. The nest is well hidden, and built by the female of moss, leaves and grass, with a lining of finer grass, hair and feathers. It can be located from ground level up to about 3m high, in a crevice or a sheltered bank, and sometimes in more unusual sites in the garden, such as discarded kettles, watering cans, flower pots, etc, and they can be attracted to nest in an open-fronted nest box. Breeding commences in March or April, with the four or five eggs incubated by the female alone for 14–16 days. After hatching, the female broods the chicks closely at first, with the male bringing food to all, after which both parents continue to tend the young until they fledge at 13–16 days. There are usually two and sometimes three broods in a year. The chicks are distinctive in having black down, and are able to merge into the shadows

when they lie prone, well camouflaged in the shady hollow of their nest.

Really quite vocal, a commonly heard call being a territorial note "tic", usually repeated as "tic-tic'tic", "pt-pt'pt" or often as "tikatik-tik", sometimes likened to the sound of an old-fashioned watch being wound up. It has a thin sharp "tseeeh", used in alarm. The song is heard throughout much of the year and frequently in autumn and winter, when resident local birds react territorially to the arrival of wintering birds from the Continent, and are often encountered singing at night around streetlights. It is a languid, melodic sequence of clear fluty whistles and rippling notes, switching between high and low frequencies and interspersed with pauses. Very variable, it typically commences with a few thin high notes, then drops into lower richer notes, often speeding up into a warbling trill and frequently including a "dee-diddlee'dee" phrase. Robins can sing at length, but phrases typically last for between 2–3 seconds, with measured pauses between.

Blackbird
Turdus merula

Length: 24–25cm
Wingspan: 34–38.5cm

JUVENILE

One of the most familiar garden birds, the Blackbird is very common and widespread and occurs in gardens in urban, suburban and rural areas. Its rich song is frequently heard as the males pronounce their territories from rooftops, aerials and garden trees, and their loud calls echo around the lanes and streets as dusk falls.

A strong-legged and sprightly ground-feeding bird, with a fairly long and broad tail. The male is uniformly black, with a bold orange-yellow bill and eye-ring. The female is almost completely dark brown, with a slightly paler central throat, faint mottling on the malar stripe and breast, blotched or spotted darker to a varying degree on the upper breast. The bill is usually brown and dull, with varying degrees of yellow-ochre showing through, with a dull yellow eye-ring. Recently-fledged juveniles have rufous tips to their body feathers, giving them a gingery appearance, while older immature birds are brown like the females, with a blackish-brown bill, the males in their first year showing a black tail and sooty plumage before acquiring their adult plumage. There are many documented cases of albinism, and it is not unusual to see Blackbirds with at least partially white plumage.

Blackbirds can be found in all types of forest and woodland with undergrowth, in farmland, scrub, copses, hedges, gardens and parks, as well as on moorland and in wetlands, provided that cover and undergrowth are available. Resident in Britain, its populations are supplemented in winter by northern and eastern birds migrating to western Europe. It often feeds on the ground under the cover of bushes and trees, where it turns over the leaf litter in search of food. Gardens provide a perfect habitat for the Blackbird, with grassy lawns offering feeding opportunities as it hunts for earthworms and insects. It will also take seeds and fruit, regularly coming to bird tables and to food scattered in open areas, although always favouring the proximity of cover to which it can retreat.

MALE

Gardens provide optimum nesting areas, with any dense bushy shrubs or trees favoured, also occasionally in a wall or building, anywhere from 1–10m off the ground and fairly well hidden. The female builds a rather large and deep nest in a fork, constructed of grass, roots, twigs etc, with a lining of mud and then a softer inner lining of finer materials. Breeding typically starts in March and April, and in a good year it can be double- or triple-brooded. The female typically lays three or four eggs, and does all the 13–14 days of incubation. The male assists in the feeding of the fledglings, which leave the nest after 14–16 days. Both adults feed the ginger-spotted youngsters for three weeks thereafter.

MALE

FEMALE

Blackbirds are rather vocal, their rich repertoire of calls making up a significant part of the soundscape of bird sounds around a typical garden. One of the loudest and therefore most familiar is the alarm call, a loud, often hysterical, tinking and clucking, as in "chink chink chink chink…" or "plih! plih! plih!", when the neighbourhood birds start 'kicking off' at dusk prior to roosting, often accelerating the calls into a manic crescendo when a bird takes flight. This call is also used in mobbing situations, and may lead the observer to find an owl roosting in the daytime. Variations include a less intense, low "chuck chuck chuck". Another more subtle but commonly heard alarm call is the 'ground predator alert' call, commonly used for cats, which is a soft "pock" or "puhc", and frequently heard when parents have fledged young and are keeping watch for danger. It also has a thin and drawn-out, descending "sseeh", given in alarm, and a more rolling "srrri", typically used on migration. The song is rich, confidently languid and pleasing, with a series of fairly low-pitched fluty notes uttered in phrases lasting 2–4 seconds, usually tailing off into low chuckling notes and often with an equal length pause between. Each male has wide variety of song phrases, sung from a prominent perch such as a roof or treetop.

FEMALE

Fieldfare
Turdus pilaris

Length: 22–27cm
Wingspan: 39–42cm

A large and rather colourful thrush, the Fieldfare has a black tail and blue-grey rump that are particularly noticeable in flight, along with its eye-catching white underwing coverts, which flash as it flies. The head and nape are grey, with blackish lores and a dark-tipped yellow bill. The underparts are white, narrowly streaked on the throat, but more heavily streaked and spotted on the breast, which is richly suffused with rusty-orange. The flanks are finely and regularly spotted, and the mantle and wing coverts are a dull maroon-brown. It can often be seen flying in loose flocks, identifiable by their chacking calls and rather languid, slightly undulating flight.

A winter visitor to Britain, it can form sizeable flocks and is most commonly found on farmland with rough fields and berry-bearing hedges. It breeds across Scandinavia and central Europe

eastwards, nesting in forest and woodland, often where open. It favours alder, birch, pine and spruce, and can also be found in montane scrub, parks, gardens, hedges and riverine belts of trees. Unless driven by hard weather, it is generally less ready to visit gardens than some of its relatives, but it may be recorded flying overhead almost anywhere. It will visit large and more rural gardens if there are berry-bearing bushes or where food – such as apples – has been put out.

Although nesting in Britain is highly unusual, breeding would commence in April or May. Unusually for a thrush, Fieldfares often nest in small colonies, in a group of adjacent trees with several nests per tree. This provides strength in numbers against predators such as crows, and they are particularly pugnacious in defending their nest against intruders, with much loud chattering and even foecal bombardment! Smaller bird species will often nest close by in order to benefit from the extra protection afforded by these feisty birds. The female

Fieldfare builds a bulky cup of mud, roots and grass, often quite high up in the fork of a tree. Five or six eggs are laid, and incubated by the female for 11–14 days. The young are tended by both parents and fledge after 12–16 days.

The song is a rather strangled and high-pitched scratchy warbling, sounding more like an undeveloped sub-song, lacking in any fluty or melodic tones. Phrases can last from 2–6 seconds, or as a continuous squeaky monologue for longer periods. The song is more emphatic when delivered in a song flight, when the bird flies level with slow and deliberate wingbeats, singing a faster warbling mixed with excited chattering. The call is a low cackling and chacking note repeated two or four times, variable in pitch and with a loose liquid quality, as in "schakk schakk schakk" or "trrruc trrruc trrruc". Migrants calling in flight often introduce a single high squeaky note. On the breeding grounds Fieldfares give a faster and more excited chatter in alarm, akin to the call of the Mistle Thrush.

Song Thrush
Turdus philomelos

Length: 21–23cm
Wingspan: 30–36cm

The Song Thrush is still a familiar garden bird for many people, despite dramatic decreases in recent decades. It can usually be seen hopping on the ground, pausing to look and listen for worms, etc. It is a compact and smallish thrush, plain brown on the upperparts and with whitish underparts that are richly suffused with yellowish-buff on the breast and flanks. It is heavily spotted with black on the underside, with black malar stripes joining up with black chevrons across the breast and down the flanks. The cheeks often show the subtle pattern of a pale patch bordered with darker smudges. It has a dark bar on the tips of the primary coverts, while the lesser and greater coverts have buff tips that form wingbars. Juveniles are similar to adults, but are more mottled in plumage and have buff streaks on the upperparts.

The Song Thrush is resident in Britain, with the population supplemented in winter by birds from northern Europe. It is found throughout the year in a wide variety of forest and woodland types, in parks and well-vegetated gardens, hedges, churchyards and smaller wooded patches, particularly where damp, and requires shade and undergrowth with adjacent open areas. It also occupies sparser island habitats and moorland. In intensively cultivated

areas where farming practices have made conditions unsuitable, gardens are an important breeding habitat. A recent study in England found that only 3.5 per cent of territories were on farmland, whereas gardens held 71.5 per cent of the territories, despite that habitat making up only two per cent of the total land area! Their favoured food is earthworms, beetles and caterpillars, as well as snails in drought or hard weather. In autumn they enjoy eating berries and fruit.

Breeding commences in late March and April, and the female builds a cup-shaped nest in a bush or tree, often close to a trunk, of twigs, grass and moss which is then plastered with mud and saliva. Four or five eggs are incubated by the female for 14–15 days, and once hatched they are tended by both parents for 14–15 days. Two or three broods per year is normal.

The loud and rich song is bold and confident, given from a tall tree or similar high position with a characteristic repetition of notes which are given three or four times and then followed by a short pause before the next sequence of notes begins, as in "errp hewp hewp hewp chu chi… trrree'ch- chi trrree'ch-chi…. peeoo peeoo peeoo… chuchich'ichichi…..do'do'di'didee… teechoo teechoo teechoo…", etc. The song is very variable, some notes being clearly enunciated and fluty, others shrill or high-pitched, and it can sometimes completely lack any pauses when the bird is singing excitedly. Calls include a thin sharp "ssip", often heard when flushed or from migrant birds, and a low scolding "chuck'chuck chuck" or "djuk djuk djuk", accelerated into a higher-pitched rattling chatter when alarmed.

Redwing
Turdus iliacus

Length: 19–22cm
Wingspan: 33–34.5cm

The Redwing is a small and attractive thrush, boldly marked with a long whitish supercilium and a whitish submoustachial stripe framing the brown ear coverts. The upperparts are uniform olive-brown, the underparts are white with a buffish wash across the breast, boldly marked with a dark malar stripe which connects to bold dark streaks and mottling on the breast and flanks. The bird takes its name from its brick-red flanks, visible when perched, and in flight it shows similarly coloured underwing coverts. It is often seen in small flocks that fly swiftly and directly, identifiable by their call and their flight profile shape, reminiscent of an ace of spades.

It is a common winter visitor to Britain, and in some years a few pairs may stay on in Scotland to breed. Commonly found in northern Europe, where it breeds in coniferous forests, as well as in mixed forest, scrub and birch. It often favours river valleys and damp areas, and will also nest in parks and gardens. In winter in Britain it is found on farmland with berry-bearing hedgerows as well as in open woodland and regularly in parks and gardens. Redwings are easily identifiable

nocturnal migrants, and on autumn and early winter nights the thin "tseep" of migrating birds can be heard overhead almost anywhere. They roost communally, and hundreds often gather at traditional sites. Dense shrubberies, hedgerows and thickets are favoured, and a good roost site will attract birds from many miles around. They will readily visit gardens if there are berry-bearing bushes, and can be attracted to apples left on the ground.

tlui-tlui", a descending "vee'du-vee'du-vee'du", a level-toned "tui-tui-tui-tui", a steeply ascending "kt'rt'tr'tr'tr'tr'tr" and a cheery "ki-chirri-chirri-chirri-chirri" delivered on a level tone, all followed by the twittering "ksch't't'rr'ttschrr'tr't'tii".

In Britain it would be a great rarity to find breeding Redwings, but they nest on or near the ground, the female building a cup-shaped structure in a bush or tree, and often close to the trunk. Four or five eggs are laid and incubated by the female for 11–15 days. The young are tended by both parents and fledge after 10–15 days, remaining dependent on the parents for a further two weeks.

The commonly heard call in Britain is uttered in flight, a thin, slightly buzzing and descending "tszeeep". It also has a soft "pok" or "chup" note, given by perched birds, a nasal "gak", and on the breeding grounds it gives a dry scolding rattle, a hard stony "trrrr trrr ktrrrr" or "trrac trrac". Migrant flocks at rest also give a collective twittering and chuckling. The song varies much between individuals, and is a loud clear sequence of three or four repeated notes lasting one or two seconds, almost always followed by a strangled, hard-to-transcribe, sub-song-like warbling and squeaking twittering phrase that lasts two or three times as long as the clear note phrase. Variants are a rising "tlui-

Mistle Thrush
Turdus viscivorus

Length: 26–29cm

Wingspan: 42–47.5cm

The Mistle Thrush is the largest and palest thrush in our region, with pallid greyish-brown upperparts, a long tail and a typically upright stance. A typical view of one would be as it hops confidently across a grassy area, such as a playing field. The sides of the head are pale whitish-buff with darker blotches on the cheek, pale lores and a bold black eye. The underparts are whitish, washed pale buffy-yellow and boldly spotted with round black spots, although more sparsely spotted than the Song Thrush. The wings are darker with pale edgings to all the feathers, the rump is paler and the darker tail has pale outer feathers and whitish spots on the tips. The underwing is white, which is very noticeable during the strong but languid, gently undulating flight.

A woodland bird, found quite widely wherever tall trees occur in conjunction with short grass, such

as in pastures, fields, parks and large gardens. The bird takes its name from its perceived love of mistletoe, although it will dominate and defend aggressively any favourite fruiting bush against other birds. It is resident in Britain, but northern European birds will move south and west in winter. Mistle Thrushes are only an occasional visitor to most gardens, as they tend to avoid enclosed areas, but they may be seen regularly in larger rural and suburban gardens with extensive lawns. They are more likely to be encountered as they fly over, giving their noisy rattling chatter, or spotted from a distance as they sing loudly from the top of a tall tree. They begin singing in the winter, when the trees are bare and they are therefore easier to spot.

Breeding commences as early as February, although more typically in March or early April. The female builds an untidy deep cup of grass, roots, moss and mud, in a tree, usually near the trunk or in a fork. Four or five eggs are laid and incubated by the female for 13–16 days, and the chicks are tended by both parents until they fledge at 14–17 days. They are fed by both parents after leaving the nest, or sometimes by just the male if the female starts another brood. Mistle Thrushes are usually double-brooded.

The song is delivered confidently from a high perch, with birds often singing in the early spring before leaves appear on the trees. Less varied and more monotonous than the song of the Blackbird, it consists of loud, unhurried clear fluty notes and gives the impression that more attention is paid to the musical composition, with pauses between phrases, such as "tchiou chew chu…trrruu tiou chu… tew chee-chu…. chewi'oo jooii…. chewi'oo jooii… tchoo'wee'di choo'ii…. choo'twee'doo choo'wi… choo wee'doowee'chu…", etc. The commonly heard call is a dry ticking rattle, often given in flight and accelerating into a more scolding sound when alarmed, such as "tschrrrrr" or "tkhrrrrrrr'r'r'r'r'r'r". It also has a rapid "tck-tck-tck".

Blackcap
Sylvia atricapilla

Length: 13.5–15cm
Wingspan: 20–23cm

One of the most common and familiar warblers in our region, the Blackcap is unmistakable and, as its name suggests, the male has a striking glossy black cap, which in the females and juveniles is rusty-brown. The cap extends down to the eye, which is rather bold and beady in an otherwise plain face, highlighted by a pale lower edge to the orbital ring. The plumage overall is a rather drab ashy-grey, browner in the female, which is sometimes confusable with the Garden Warbler if the head is not seen. Although quite skulking at times, it is fairly robust and often draws attention to itself as it moves about in the bushes.

It is primarily a summer visitor, arriving from Africa at the beginning of April. In recent years, however, some central European birds have taken to wintering in gardens in southern England, and so they may be encountered here throughout the year. Presumably the ready availability of food, particularly from bird tables, and the avoidance of migration over the Alps, compensate for the less than ideal climate. During the breeding season their diet chiefly comprises insects, changing to fruits such as raspberry, cherry, currants, elder and bramble in late summer and during autumn migration. Overwinterers feed on fat, bread, peanuts, cheese, porridge oats, potato and coconut.

Studies have shown that those birds wintering in England tend to mate only among themselves, and not usually with those wintering in the Mediterranean. This is because the short-

FEMALE

Four or five eggs are laid and incubated by both sexes for 13–14 days. The young fledge after 11–12 days.

The call is a rather clear and loud clicking "teck", repeated several times when anxious. It also has a low churring "dzrrrr", and a bleating "schweehh" call when alarmed or distressed. It is quite vocal, and has a loud and distinctive cheery song consisting of a rich warbling that breaks into a louder, clearer and rather strident fluty song phrase. The initial warbling may cause confusion with the song of the Garden Warbler, but the Blackcap should burst forth into the loud terminal flourish part of the song, whereas the Garden Warbler maintains the same level of intensity throughout. The loud part of the song is usually 2–4 seconds long, but the initial warbling can carry on for much longer.

MALE

distance migrants arrive back from the wintering grounds for breeding earlier than birds wintering around the Mediterranean, and of course may have spent the winter together, when pair-bonds are initiated. In the breeding season Blackcaps favour shady woodland with rich undergrowth, in mixed or deciduous forest, thickets, parks, overgrown gardens, hedges and dense bushy areas. They are very arboreal, singing from taller bushes and trees.

Breeding usually commences in late April or May, with the female building a neat compact cup in a dense bush or tree, constructed of grass, roots and stems, and complete with 'handles' attaching it to supporting stems.

MALE

Garden Warbler
Sylvia borin

Length: 13–14.5cm
Wingspan: 20–24.5cm

A demure and unassuming bird, its most obvious feature is the lack of any major plumage features! Furthermore, it is rather secretive and often not detected except by its song or calls. It is rather plump and stocky, with a rounded head, plain mouse-brown upperparts and whitish underparts that are washed browner on the flanks. The tail is plain and lacks white outer feathers. The dark, staring eye is obvious, with pale crescents above and below, and set in a gentle-looking face. The bill is fairly stout and pale grey on the lower mandible, and the stout legs are light grey. The sexes are alike, and juveniles appear very similar to adults.

The Garden Warbler is a summer visitor, breeding in mixed and deciduous open woodland with clearings and rich undergrowth, in parks, large gardens, streamside woods, thickets and heaths. It requires taller trees mixed with shrubbery, and so has much habitat overlap with Blackcap, but generally favours more shrubby areas. The songs of the two species are so similar that they create mutually exclusive territories. Since Blackcaps arrive on breeding grounds before Garden Warblers, this

prevents the Garden Warblers from occupying some suitable sites. However, if the Blackcaps are experimentally removed, Garden Warblers will move in to occupy their territories. Despite its name, it is not an obvious garden bird, but may frequent large gardens where the appropriate breeding habitat is present. It can also turn up in gardens in late summer and autumn, when it switches from an insect-rich diet to one of fruit, especially elderberry and blackberry, both of which are high in energy and so help fuel its southward migration.

Breeding commences in May, and both sexes build a rather loose and bulky cup of dry grass and rootlets in a dense bush, wedged but not attached to adjacent branches. The male will also build various 'trial' nests before the final one is selected. Four or five eggs are laid, and incubated for 11–13 days by both sexes. The young are tended by both sexes and fly the nest after 10–13 days, but will stay with the female for longer.

The song is a very pleasant, confident sweet baritone warbling, sustained for 3–8 seconds, rising and falling throughout the song phrase. Although similar to that of the Blackcap, and often confused with it, the Garden Warbler's song is quicker, more subdued, has a mellower sound and is often sung in longer phrases and without the sudden changes in pitch towards the end. It descends into lower frequency notes more often than the Blackcap, and was once described as "having taken singing lessons from a brook passing under a small bridge"! The call is a rather nasal chacking sound and is often repeated in a series of calls, particularly when anxious, such as "djeck djeck djeck…". It also has a low grating "chrrrr" and a soft ascending "duij", given in alarm.

Lesser Whitethroat

Sylvia curruca

Length: 11.5–13.5cm

Wingspan: 16.5–20.5cm

Another rather anonymous and unspectacular bird, this is a smallish and compact warbler with dull grey-brown upperparts. The key feature to look out for is the dark grey ear coverts, which are distinctly darker than the rest of the cap and contrast with the white throat. Some individuals may show a narrow white line over the forehead and bill. Its tail, grey-brown with white outer tail feathers, is shorter than in the Common Whitethroat. The wing is plain and without any rufous or pale panels, the underparts are dull whitish and washed browner on the sides. The bill is fairly short and grey with a paler base, and the legs are dark grey. Juveniles are essentially similar to adults, although they tend to be browner with a less contrasting head pattern. A little more secretive than the Common Whitethroat, the best way to locate this bird is by its voice.

A summer visitor, favouring taller vegetation than the Common Whitethroat and mainly found in bushy areas between woodland and open country, such as in mature farmland hedgerows,

heathland, plantations, well-grown gardens, parks and cemeteries, woodland edge and clearings, scrub and thickets. It occurs more widely on passage, when birds may appear in any kind of bushy area. They can be found in large gardens offering suitable habitat and, like several of their close relatives, may be seen feeding on blackberries and other fruit in autumn. It is unique amongst British birds in that it migrates around and across the eastern side of the Mediterranean (to its winter quarters in north-eastern Africa), rather than taking the more direct southwards route.

Breeding commences in May, and four or five eggs are laid in a loose cup built of grass, twigs and roots and cobwebs and positioned low in a dense bush. The female will begin construction of the nest, the male adding some final adornments of hair or cobwebs. The eggs are incubated for 11–12 days by both male and female, and both

sexes feed the young, which leave the nest after 12–13 days when they are only just able to flutter.

The call is a hard and dry, tongue-clicking "tekk" or "thekk", often repeated freely. It also has a hoarse grating churr, and an alarmed rattle similar to that of the Wren. The song is a distinctive hard wooden rattling, reminiscent of part of the song of the Chaffinch, and is made up of 6–12 double notes at a rate of roughly 10 per second, a "djeh'djeh'djeh'djeh'djeh'djeh". A weak and subdued warbling of varying length usually precedes this rattle, and longer variants can sound similar to the warbling of the Blackcap or Common Whitethroat. It starts quietly and builds up in volume to the louder rattle part, with the quiet introduction often only audible at close range. It can sometimes deliver these two parts of the song separately. There is no song flight, unlike the Common Whitethroat, and there can be quite a variation in song across their wide range.

Common Whitethroat
Sylvia communis

Length: 13–15cmcm

Wingspan: 18.5–23cm

The Whitethroat is a fairly common and well-known hedgerow bird, although numbers seem to fluctuate from year to year. In 1968 it suffered a major population crash from which it has yet to recover fully. The most likely cause of this drop in numbers was a drought in the western Sahel region of Africa, where these migrants spend part of the winter.

This is a sturdy and large-headed warbler with a fairly long, white-sided tail. The male has a greyish head, a white orbital ring and a grey-brown back,

and in all plumages shows broad bright rufous margins to the black-centred secondaries, tertials and wing coverts. The underparts are whitish, with pure white on the throat contrasting with a pink flush on the breast. The female is browner, washed buff on the breast, with a brown head, a pale orbital ring and a pale brown eye. Juveniles are similar to females but have a darker eye and a browner tail with sandy-buff outer tail-feathers.

It is a summer visitor to our region, the first males turning up in April and the females arriving 7–10 days afterwards. Whitethroats favour scrubby places in a wide range of habitats, such as farmland with hedges, tall herbage, crops, low bushes, bramble thickets, shrubby margins of wetlands, open woodland clearings and forest edge, from sunny lowland areas to upland hillsides. Generally confiding and curious, it will often pose on the tops of bushes in order to investigate anyone approaching. While not a typical garden visitor, like other Sylvia warblers it enjoys feeding on fruit in the autumn and may be seen in large untidy

MALE

lively rapid warble, quite shrill and scratchy, delivered from a raised perch, or a little longer, richer, and more fluid when given in a jerky little song flight. In its simplest version it is just 1–1.5 seconds long, with 6–12-note components, such as an easy-to-remember "witchetty-witchetty-witchetty-witch!" or, more accurately, as "weech'u-cheh'weh-i'chu-chi'chiih!", often slightly descending through the sequence, ascending sometimes on the final two or three notes. Longer and more complex versions can last up to 10 seconds or more, and sound more warbling and similar to other Sylvia species.

MALE IN DISPLAY FLIGHT

gardens with bramble thickets, or where a garden is adjacent to its favoured habitat.

Breeding commences in early May. The nest is a deep grassy cup, built low down in a low bush or in tall herbage, and the male will build several trial nests before the female chooses one, or they build another one together. Four to five eggs are laid and incubated by both sexes for 12–13 days, and the young are tended by both parents and fledge after 12–14 days.

Quite vocal, with a range of call notes, such as a nervous nasal "dverhr dverhr dverhr" and a low "dzhuurrr", a lively "whit-whit-whit" which often precedes song, and a sharp, often repeated "tak". The song is a brisk and

IMMATURE/1ST WINTER

Chiffchaff
Phylloscopus collybita

Length: 10–12cm

Wingspan: 15–21cm

This plain little warbler is one of the first common summer visitors to arrive in Britain. Its distinctive song can be heard from March onwards, when birds are easiest to see as they sing from the bare treetops. They are quite confiding, and have a distinctive habit of flicking their wings and dipping the tail. Very similar to the Willow Warbler, they are best separated by voice, but at all ages a non-vocal bird can be distinguished by its dark brown or blackish legs. The overall coloration is more olive-brown than the Willow Warbler, with less yellow tones in the plumage. The underparts are off-white, with a variable amount of yellow-buff washing on the throat and breast. The facial 'expression' is subtly different, the Chiffchaff having a less strongly marked face than the Willow Warbler and with a more indistinct supercilium and the darker cheeks highlighting the whitish eye-ring, which is bisected by a dark eyestripe. It is also slightly dumpier and shorter-winged.

The males are among the first arrivals in spring, when they set up territories some two or three weeks before the females arrive. Chiffchaffs favour rather tall trees, and can be found in open mixed and deciduous woodland with tall trees in combination with shrubs and ground cover, in large gardens, parks, churchyards, tall hedgerows, tall scrub and plantations.

Outside the breeding season they are less tied to taller trees, and are found in a wider range of habitats. They are likely to nest in large untidy gardens or visit for feeding, although, being insectivorous, they will not use feeders. Many overwinter in milder parts of

southern Britain, appearing in sheltered gardens along the south coast in particular.

Breeding commences in April and May. The female builds a domed nest with a side entrance, either on the ground or low in undergrowth, and made of dead leaves, grass and moss, and thickly lined with feathers. Five or six eggs are laid and incubated by the female for 13–14 days. The male has little involvement in the nesting process other than defending the territory, and the chicks are fed mostly by the female until they fledge after 14–16 days. After fledging, the young stay in the vicinity of the nest for three to four weeks, and are fed by and roost with the female. Two broods in a season is usual.

The call is a simpler, more monosyllabic and higher-pitched version of the Willow Warbler's call, a slightly upwards-inflected and emphatic "huitt", "pwee!" or "h'weet". When anxious it will give a flatter "peep", and juveniles make a similar call. The eponymous song is a rather slow and measured, monotonous clear two-note repetition, the first note higher than the second, as in "tsilf-tsalf tsilf-tsalf tsilf-tsalf….", often ending on a lower note. It occasionally elaborates on this simple rhythm with variations, such as a three-note "chiff-chiff'chaff, chiff-chiff-chaff chiff-chiff-chaff…". Between bouts of song it often gives a "trrrr… trrrr…" sound, audible only at fairly close range. It often sings from high in a tall tree.

Willow Warbler
Phylloscopus trochilus

Length: 11–12.5cm
Wingspan: 16.5–22cm

ADULT
SPRING
PLUMAGE

A small, slim and restless warbler, this demure little bird is unusual in that it moults all its feathers twice per year, once on the breeding grounds and then again in its winter quarters, a feature perhaps related to its long migration between northern Europe and southern Africa. It is most similar in appearance and behaviour to the Chiffchaff, and best separated by voice, but at all ages a non-vocal bird can be identified by its pinkish-brown legs. It is greyish-green with a hint of brown on the upperparts, and the underparts are whitish with a pale yellow wash on the throat and breast. The face is well marked, with a long pale yellow supercilium and a well-defined dark eyestripe. The wings show quite a long primary projection, giving it a slightly

JUVENILE
AUTUMN
PLUMAGE

FLYCATCHING

elongated shape. Immatures in autumn can be quite striking and are suffused with a brighter yellow on the whole of the underparts and the face.

A common summer visitor, found in a wide variety of bushy habitats. It favours open woodland, both deciduous and coniferous, birch forest, willow scrub, heaths, commons, plantations, parks, large gardens, indeed virtually anywhere where there are shrubs and small trees, preferring younger growth than that favoured by the similar Chiffchaff. Its range extends right up into the higher latitudes and beyond the Arctic Circle. As a garden bird, it may visit or even nest in a rural or large suburban garden, or be found feeding there during its post-breeding dispersal or migration.

Breeding commences in May, and the nest is usually on the ground where there are trees with lots of ground cover beneath. The female builds a domed structure of grass, stems and moss, and with a side entrance. Five to seven eggs are laid at

daily intervals, and are incubated for 13–14 days by the female only. The chicks are fed by both parents and fledge after 13–16 days.

The call is a rather soft, plaintive, enquiring, disyllabic and upwards-inflected "hoo-eet", the second syllable higher than the first. It can also give a more monotone "hwuu" version of the call when anxious, and a repeated nasal scolding "chwherr" when alarmed near the nest, not unlike that of a *Sylvia* warbler. The song is a pleasing cadence of simple whistles descending through the scales, such as "svi'svi'svi'svi tue-tue-tue-tuee hweh-hweh-hweeo-hweo-hweo hi'hi-hiwe'oo". The initial three or four notes are slightly faster, sharper and higher, followed by 8–10 notes which are given quite strongly and descend the scale in steps. The final notes sound weaker and more stifled, tailing off at the end, although this is variable. The song generally lasts between 2–3 seconds, or in longer phrases of up to 4.5 seconds.

Goldcrest
Regulus regulus

Length: 8.5–9.5cm
Wingspan: 13.5–15.5cm

Our tiniest bird, weighing as little as 5g! It is dumpy and rotund, with a large head, a thin blackish bill and a pale-ringed beady black eye set in an otherwise plain face. It is pale green on the upperparts, with a bold wing pattern of a broad whitish bar on the tips of the greater coverts and primary coverts, contrasting with a black bar on the base of the secondaries. The crown is yellow in the centre, mixed with flame-orange in the male, and bordered on each side with bold black lines. The male's crest is raised and spread sideways during courtship, as well as during aggressive displays towards other males. Juveniles are similar to adults but are duller and have a plain head, totally lacking any crown markings.

Resident in our region, but with northern breeders migrating south in winter to supplement resident populations. Although easily overlooked due to its small size and habit of keeping high in the branches, it is common and widespread throughout Britain and north-western Europe, and can be located easily once the calls are learned. In the breeding season it favours mixed and coniferous woodland, as well as parks and gardens, especially where conifers are present. At other times it ranges more widely, and can be found in deciduous woodland and almost

FEMALE
WITH
CHICKS

MALE

any kind of wooded or bushy area, often joining feeding flocks of tits. In October immigrants arrive in variable numbers on the east coast of Britain, when they can be found in coastal scrub before they dispersing inland.

Breeding commences in April or May, and the nest is built by both sexes. Constructed of moss, lichen and spider webs, it is suspended hammock-like below a branch in a conifer. A clutch is typically six to eight eggs, but occasionally as many as 12 are laid – an extraordinary number constituting 150 per cent of the female's body weight! She incubates the eggs for 16–19 days, and both parents feed the chicks. Fledging occurs after 17–18 days, and two broods per season are usual. Sometimes the male constructs a second nest while the female is incubating the first clutch. When the chicks hatch, the female lays a second clutch in the second nest and begins incubating that one, while the male takes over the duties of feeding the first brood!

The calls and song of the Goldcrest are very high-pitched, between 7–8kHz, and sadly for older birders they are one of the first common bird sounds that are lost when hearing begins to deteriorate. The common call is a thin, three- or four-note "sszi-sszi-sszi-sszi", often used as a contact call, as well as a rather more shrill and stronger-sounding "zzit-zzit-zzit", also given singly and occasionally sounding a little rough and hoarse. It also gives random little high-pitched "zze" sounds when feeding. The song is a rapid shuttling high-pitched sequence, the main phrase repeated with a cyclical quality and finished off with a variable lower-pitched trilling flourish, such as "ti'wii'titoo-wii'titoo-wii'titoo-wii'titoo zee'ti't'trrrrreo".

Spotted Flycatcher
Muscicapa striata

Length: 13.5–15cm

Wingspan: 23–25.5cm

A good example of a poorly named bird, as it is streaked rather than spotted! Small and slim, it sits upright on short black legs, making quick sallies after insects from an exposed perch and often returning to the same branch. It has long wings, which are flicked nervously while perched, when it also pumps its tail. Lacking any obvious

plumage features, it is grey-brown on the head and upperparts, faintly streaked and spotted darker on the fore-crown. It has a plain face with a beady black eye and a thin, broad-based black bill. The underparts are whitish, with indistinct mottled streaking on the throat sides and breast.

A summer visitor that is widespread but declining in Britain, with nest predation by Grey Squirrels a possible contributory factor. It is a bird of forest edge, favouring tall deciduous trees around clearings and glades that offer flycatching perches and adjacent open airspace. It is also sometimes found in pine and larch, and often occurs in manmade habitats offering suitable conditions, such as parks, large gardens, avenues of tall trees, orchards and churchyards. Flying insects are the main diet, although berries are also taken, especially in the autumn.

The first birds arrive in May and breeding commences soon after. Both sexes take part in the building of a loose cup-shaped nest made of grass and other vegetable matter and lined with feathers, hair and dead leaves, located in a suitable recess in a tree or against a wall. Where breeding is succesful, they return year after year to the same niche and in some cases the same nest is repaired and re-used. They will adapt readily to an open-fronted nest box, which is often a good way of attracting them to a garden. The incubation is done solely by the female, who lays four or five eggs. These hatch after 13–15 days, and at first the male brings food to the female while she broods the chicks, after which both parents attend the young. The young fledge after 13–16 days, and continue to be fed by the parents for another three weeks; newly fledged young usually roost together on a branch. Spotted Flycatchers are

sometimes double-brooded and, unlike many European birds, are able to discriminate between their own eggs and those of other species – a good defence against Cuckoos, which do not appear to nest-parasitize them.

The song is a quiet, very simple and primitive series of single high-pitched squeaks and strangled sounds, delivered at a rate of one note per 0.7–1.5 seconds with regular pauses in between, and with no formation of phrases like other flycatchers, as in "u'ii.. tzii.. tzi'i.. pzzt.. pzzt.. tzhrr.. tzhrr.. tz'i… u'ii.. u'ii.. tzu.. tzu.. u'ii.. u'ii..", etc. The call is also rather unobtrusive, a short shrill "zee", not unlike the calls of the Robin and Hawfinch. The alarm call, often given near the nest, is a combination of this call and a couple of hard tacking notes, such as "zee'thk" or "zee'thk'thk". It also makes some loud bill-snapping sounds, often rapid and sounding rattle-like.

JUVENILE

Pied Flycatcher
Ficedula hypoleuca

Length: 12–13.5cm
Wingspan: 21.5–24cm

This delightful bird is most eye-catching in spring, when it arrives on its breeding grounds in a flurry of nuptial activity. It has a compact

FEMALE AT NESTBOX

shape and a habit of nervously flicking its tail up when perched. The male is strikingly plumaged, with a black back, head and wings (often tinged brownish), a black tail with white on the basal half of the outer feathers, and a large white patch on the base of the secondaries and half of the tertials. The underparts are pure white, and there is a small white patch over the bill. Females and immatures are more demure, tawny grey-brown above, darker on the wings and tail, and with a white patch on the tertials and a white band on the tips of the greater coverts. It does not share the Spotted Flycatcher's habit of continually returning to the same flycatching perch.

A summer visitor, in Britain the Pied Flycatcher has a marked westerly distribution and is particularly attracted to insect-rich sessile oakwoods in hilly country. Elsewhere in its range it can be found in mixed or deciduous forest with glades and clearings, with the availability of nest holes being an important factor. It is also found in avenues, orchards and parks, and sometimes in large gardens containing, or adjacent to, suitable habitat. In Scandinavia it is also found nesting in towns and adapts well where nest boxes are provided, which may even be a significant factor in local population increases in Britain. It can be found more widely on passage, and it is not impossible for a migrant to appear in a garden, particularly in coastal areas.

The female builds a loose cup of plant material, moss and feathers in the nest cavity, while the male sings sweetly nearby. Six or seven eggs are laid and incubated by the female alone for 13–15 days. The young are fed by both parents, although mainly

JUVENILE AUTUMN
PLUMAGE

by the female, and fledge after 16–17 days.

The calls are an insistent and frequently repeated "bidt!", a loud, penetrating Chaffinch-like "whit", and a short "ttuc", sometimes given together with the previous call to make "whit-ttuc". In alarm it will give a Chiffchaff-like "wheet". The advertising song of the male is a simple but confident phrase of 7–12 notes, typically lasting between 1.5–3 seconds, as in "tsi'chu tsi'chu tsi'chu tsi'tsi'tsi'che", the repeated introductory notes always constant, the later ones variable from one song phrase to the next and often delivered in a little flourish. It is reminiscent of the song of the Common Redstart, but slower and more evenly paced. A less well-structured, more strangled and excited variant is given when the male has attracted a female to a potential nest.

ADULT MALE SPRING
PLUMAGE

Long-tailed Tit
Aegithalos caudatus

Length: 13–15cm (inc. tail of 7–9cm)
Wingspan: 16–19cm

A cute little 'lollipop' of a bird, with a small body and very long tail. Round-headed, and with a tiny black bill, it is often seen moving in restless flocks with a weak bouncing flight, playing follow-my-leader across gaps in trees and along hedgerows. The head and underparts are whitish with a broad black band that runs from in front of the eye along the side of the crown to the nape, and faint black streaks on the cheek. The upperparts are black, with a large panel of dirty pink on the scapulars. The tail is black with white on the outer feathers, and the short stubby wings have broad white edges on the tertials and secondaries. Juveniles are browner than the adults, with more extensive dark markings on the head, and the pink areas of plumage are whiter. Northern populations of the nominate race have a completely snowy-white head.

The Long-tailed Tit is resident and found rather commonly across Britain, however northern populations occasionally undergo irruptions southwards. It favours deciduous and mixed woodland, with plenty of thick undergrowth such as hazel and willow, and is also found in scrub and bushy areas away from woodland, such as in gardens, parks, hedges in farmland and other marginal habitats with secondary growth. Frequently found in small flocks that keep together with constant contact calls, they can be quite fearless and inquisitive. These groups are often family parties, and birds can be seen zipping back and forwards, trying to keep together if one or more members of the party drop out of line. They occur often in gardens, travelling through in active feeding flocks, or even nesting within undisturbed corners. They are

strongly insectivorous, but will visit feeders to take advantage of fat cakes, seed mixes and peanuts.

The nest is an oval, domed structure built from moss and bound together with spider webs, coated with lichen on the outside and lined with feathers. It is usually placed in a fork in a dense or thorny bush, and is built by both adults. Breeding commences in April, and six to eight eggs are laid, with the female doing the majority of the incubation for 15–18 days, the male bringing food to her. Both parents feed the young, but occasionally they will have 'helpers' assisting the feeding, possibly involving related individuals whose own nest has failed. Fledging occurs after 16–17 days.

A noisy and vocal bird, frequently heard uttering a thin and weak-sounding "ssi'ssi'ssi'ssi" when in flight or as a contact note. This call is easy to mimic and they often respond by coming very close to the observer to investigate. Another commonly heard call is a dry and slurred "trrrr", and short little conversational "pt" note. It also gives a harder scolding "tsrr'r'r'r'r" when excited or alarmed, and an agitated and alert-sounding "tsrrr-tsrrr". Infrequently heard, the song is a rather random and hurried collection of short, dry chipping notes, interspersed with nasal twittering and bubbling sounds and a few short melodious whistles.

JUVENILES

Blue Tit
Cyanistes caeruleus

Length: 10.5–12cm
Wingspan: 17.5–20cm

One of the most common and familiar garden birds, the Blue Tit is very small and lightweight with primrose-yellow underparts. It has a rounded head patterned with broad white cheeks, a white forehead and white extending in a ring around

JUVENILE

to the nape, isolating a rounded crown patch of blue. It has a blackish bridle through the eye, separating cheek from crown, and a darker blue collar-ring below the cheek, broadest at the rear and joining a blackish-blue chin and throat at the front. The mantle is green, and the wings and tail are blue with white tertial tips and a white wingbar on the tips of the greater coverts. Females are duller than males, and they are thought to select those partners that have the brightest caps, which glow brightly when seen in the ultra-violet spectrum. Juveniles are greenish-brown on the upper-parts and have yellow cheeks.

A common resident, it favours deciduous or mixed woodland and forest, parks, gardens, orchards, hedges, scrub, and indeed any bushy areas with scattered trees, wherever it can find a ready food supply and holes to nest in. It is a familiar visitor to garden bird feeders, especially in the winter months, when it also readily joins roaming mixed flocks.

Breeding commences in April, and both sexes build a nest of moss and hair inside the selected cavity. An average of 8–10 eggs are then laid and incubated by the female for 13–15 days, while the male brings food to her. The chicks are tended by both adults and fledge after 18–21 days, and follow the parents for some time after leaving the nest. Usually there is just one brood. Blue Tit broods are vulnerable to being 'cleaned-out' by various predators such as Grey Squirrels and Great Spotted Woodpeckers.

A commonly used call is a churring note, which starts low and rises in a short rolling trill, and is delivered in various permutations, such as "chwrrr'r'r'r'r'r", "chwrr'hi'ih'ih" or "twr'r'r'i'i'i'i'i", or commencing with high notes before dropping sharply, as in "tsii'tsii'tsii-chwrr'r'r'r'r". It uses a more scolding "trrrrr-bii'beep!" and a drawn-out "seeer" in response to aerial predators, a conversational high-pitched "tsee" when in a group, and a repeated drier note, "di'di'di'di". Song variants include a repeated high-pitched, clear silvery "bii'bi-sisisi-srr'r'r'r'r'r'r'r, bii'bi-sisisi-srr'r'r'r'r'r'r'r, bii'bi-sisisi-srr'r'r'r'r'r'r'r'r" and a high, cyclical and buzzing "tsee-zzi'zi, tzii'zi'zee- tzii'zi'zee-tzii'zi'zee- tzii'zi'zee".

During the breeding season it will feed on insects and caterpillars, and is an important species in the control of garden pests such as aphids. It is famous for its ability to learn how to open foil-capped milk bottles, to get at the cream in the top of the bottle, but this habit is seen much less these days with the reduction in doorstep deliveries and rise in the popularity of low-fat milk. It readily occupies nest boxes and can be further encouraged to take up residence in gardens by the provision of these; otherwise it can use any kind of hole, either natural or in some artificial structure.

Great Tit
Parus major

Length: 13.5–15cm
Wingspan: 22.5–25.5cm

The largest tit in the region and a very familiar garden bird, the Great Tit has an ebullient nature and striking plumage. The underparts are bright yellow, bisected by a bold black stripe running from throat to vent. The belly stripe on a male Great Tit is an indicator of his status, and females are attracted to males with bigger stripes. The head and throat are glossy black with a large white cheek patch that is fully enclosed. The mantle is green, and the wings are slaty-blue with a broad white wingbar on the tips of the greater coverts. The tail is quite long, grey-blue and with white outer feathers. Females are slightly less bright than the males and have a narrower black belly stripe; juveniles appear duller and washed out, with yellowish cheeks and a brown cap.

A common resident, it is found in similar habitats to the Blue Tit, such as deciduous and mixed woodland, sometimes in coniferous forest, plus hedges, thickets, parks, churchyards, gardens and virtually any area with scattered trees, shrubs and bushes. It is primarily a lowland bird, although it can occur up to the treeline in mountainous areas. It adapts well to the presence of man and is a regular visitor to bird feeders. It is insectivorous during the breeding season, preferring to feed its young on protein-rich caterpillars, and studies have shown that Great Tits have a significant impact in reducing

tii-twerr". It commonly utters a low purring or scolding, slightly rising "tchr'r'r'r'r'r", which can be combined with higher-pitched calls such as "tii'tii'wrrrrr". The song is also highly variable, but typically is a repeated series of two or three loud, clear and ringing notes repeated in a 'see-sawing' style for 3–10 times, though often just four or five. Studies have identified that Great Tits with the broadest repertoire of songs will be more successful in defending their territories, which is why they use so many different variations. These are just some of the many possible examples: "dti'too dti'too dti'too dti'too dti'too", "pu'tingk pu'tingk pu'tingk pu'tingk", "chi'wer chi'wer chi'wer chi'wer chi'wer", "ba'ba'ding-ba'ba'ding-ba'ba'ding-ba'ba'ding", and the classic "tea'cher tea'cher tea'cher tea'cher".

caterpillar damage in apple orchards. In autumn they will eat fruit, and in winter they switch to nuts and seeds. Like the Blue Tit, they have the ability to break the foil caps of milk bottles to plunder the cream floating on top.

The nest is in a hole of some kind, either natural or in an artificial structure (it readily uses nest boxes), and is built by the female of moss, roots, grass and spider webs, lined with down and feathers. Breeding commences in April and seven to nine eggs are laid. The female incubates for 13–15 days, while the male brings food to her. The chicks fledge after 18–21 days, and continue to be fed by the parents for another couple of weeks.

The Great Tit is highly vocal, with many different calls, often with a clear ringing bell-like quality. Variants include a "psi! ping ping", a Chaffinch-like "pink-pink", and a "tii-twerr,

Coal Tit
Periparus ater

Length: 10–11.5cm

Wingspan: 17–21cm

A small short-tailed tit with a small fine bill, this is a common but rather furtive bird compared to some of its relatives. It has a big boldly marked head, with a black cap that extends onto the nape, framing an oblong white nape-patch that serves as its most distinct field mark. The cheeks are white, and there is a large amount of black on the throat, flaring out onto the shoulder where it breaks up into black flecking. The underparts are whitish-buff, more strongly coloured on the flanks. There are white spots on the tips of the greater and median coverts, forming a double wingbar. Juveniles are drabber than the adults but have all the white parts of the plumage washed yellow to varying degrees. Various races occur within our region; the British race has an olive-grey mantle and wings, whereas birds on Continental Europe have a blue-grey mantle and wings. Coal Tits are highly agile, acrobatic and restless, and although they join mixed feeding flocks outside the breeding season, they are generally more solitary by nature.

It is a resident in our region, although in some years northern populations may head southwards in large numbers. It is a bird of conifer forest and is found at a wide range of altitudes. It has a preference for spruce, but also occurs widely in mixed forest and in some parts of its range can be found in pure deciduous woods. It is common in parks and large

BRITISH
RACE

CONTINENTAL
RACE

gardens, almost always where conifers are present – Coal Tit numbers have expanded with the spread of conifer plantations. It ranges widely in winter, joining mixed flocks and often visiting both seed and nut feeders in gardens.

They will use nest boxes, but otherwise their favoured nesting sites are a hole in a tree or in a rotting tree-stump, and sometimes on the ground in a bank. The nest is built by both sexes and is constructed of moss and spider webs. Breeding commences in April or May and usually 9–10 eggs are laid, although sometimes as many as 12. Incubation is by the female for 14–16 days, and both parents tend the young. They fledge after 16–19 days, and sometimes there is a second brood.

The song is a rapid, rather high-pitched repetition of a clear double note, reminiscent of the song of the Great Tit but delivered at a brisker pace and sounding sweeter and 'tighter', as in "pew-ti-tew ti-tew ti-tew ti-tew ti-tew-pi", "tii'cher tii'cher tii'cher tii'cher tii'cher" or "ti'chew ti'chew ti'chew ti'chew ti'chew", or a more trisyllabic "too'i'tee too'i'tee too'i'tee too'i'tee..". Individual songsters can give a wide variety of versions, all sung on the same basic theme but differing in rhythm, pace and emphasis. It gives many different calls; a frequently heard one is a twanging "tyu'ii" or "ti'duu'ii", or a monosyllabic "tuuy", but it also has high-pitched conversational calls such as a sharp "psitt, psitt" and a shivering Goldcrest-like "tss'ss'ss'ss'ii".

Willow Tit
Poecile montanus

Length: 12–13cm
Wingspan: 17–20.5cm

The Willow Tit is a very similar bird to the Marsh Tit, and much care is required in separating the two species. The voice is often the easiest way to tell them apart.

In terms of physical characteristics, the Willow shares the same black cap, white cheek and brown upperparts as the Marsh, but the head is rather bigger, and it has a matt instead of a glossy black cap, as well as a more extensive black bib that tends to be more triangular in shape. The most obvious plumage difference is a pale panel on the closed wing, formed by the pale edgings to the secondaries, tertials and greater coverts, and a feature lacking in the Marsh. The underparts are buffish-white, with warm buff on the flanks, subtly richer in colour than on the Marsh. In Scandinavia Willow Tits are colder and greyer with whiter cheeks, and are therefore much more distinctive.

Resident and sedentary across the region, but in serious decline in many parts of Britain, with a 50 per cent drop in numbers between

1972–96. Although they may suffer in cold winters, it is possible that this decline is related more to competition with the commoner tit species, which benefit from the erection of nest boxes. In the north of its range the Willow Tit favours coniferous forest, but in Britain it can be found in deciduous and mixed woodland, with a preference for damp or marshy woods with willow, alder, elder and birch, hedgerows, copses, and scrub in overgrown marshes, with a supply of the dead or rotting wood that it requires for breeding. While this is perhaps no longer a typical visitor to gardens, where localized populations occur it may visit a rural or unkempt suburban garden if suitable habitat is nearby, and it will occasionally use bird feeders.

The nest is built by both sexes in decaying wood that is soft enough for them to excavate a hole, although they will also use existing holes. The nest is made of a sparse amount of down, wood chips and fibres, and breeding commences in April or May. An average of six to eight eggs are laid, the female incubating for 13–15 days while the male brings food to her. Both parents tend the young, for 17–20 days.

The call is the best way to tell it from the similar Marsh Tit, and is usually a sequence of two different notes. The first is a high, short "zzi", repeated just once or twice; the second is a hoarse nasal drawn-out note, such as "zzi'zi djaeeer djaeer djaeer djaeer". Often just the "djaeer" notes are given, and this is used as a contact call or given more excitedly in alarm. It also gives some short "chup" or "chit" notes, and some short typically tit-like high-pitched "sit" calls. The main song type is a series of three to five loud, downwardly-inflected piping whistles, as in "tiou'tiou'tiou'tiou'tiou". Another song, but rarely heard, is a collection of sweet, rather strangled and subdued warbling phrases, plus a Greenfinch-like rattle.

Marsh Tit
Poecile palustris

Length: 11.5–13cm
Wingspan: 18–19.5cm

Although still not uncommon in many areas, this species declined in numbers by more than 60 per cent between 1960 and 2000. It is a compact, large-headed and dumpy-bodied tit, most likely to be confused with the Willow Tit, to which it is very similar. Their calls are a sure way to separate the two, but otherwise care must be taken over identification. The Marsh has a neat glossy black cap that extends to the nape in a narrow line, bordering a large whitish cheek. It has a small black bill and a small black 'bib', or chin and upper throat, typically much smaller than on the Willow Tit. The upperparts are uniform mouse-brown, without any pale panel on the wing. The tail is brown, and the underparts are whitish, washed buff on the flanks. The sexes are similar, and the juveniles look similar to the adults but show a sooty black crown, adding further confusion with the Willow Tit!

Resident and widespread throughout much of England and Europe, it is found in deciduous and mixed woodland, with a preference for oak and beech. It prefers a moist habitat, and can also be found in alder carr, riverine trees and shrubs at the margins of wetland, ideally with dead or decaying trees, as it requires ready-made holes for nesting. 'Marsh' Tit is a misleading name, for although the bird is found in damp and marshy places, it is as common in dry woods and hedgerows and also found in parks and large gardens where suitable broad-leaved vegetation occurs. It will often visit feeders

and bird tables, and also joins winter mixed tit flocks, although usually only in ones and twos; pure flocks of this species are unlikely. Unlike most other tits, this bird has been observed to store the food for the winter, by tucking in seeds behind tree bark or in similar semi-hidden places.

Marsh Tits will use nest boxes occasionally, but prefer natural nest holes in a stump or tree, such as in ash, elder or willow where holes may develop in a knot on the trunk. It may modify an existing hole to suit, and the nest is built by the female of moss, hair and feathers, while the male accompanies and encourages her. Breeding commences in late April, and seven to nine eggs are laid. The female incubates the eggs for 14–16 days and, once hatched, she will brood the young chicks for 9–10 days. Both parents

take part in feeding the young, which fledge after 18–21 days, and will continue to feed them for a week after they have flown the nest.

The diagnostic call is a quick, explosive "pssi'chew!" or "ssi'ssi'chew", often followed by and combined with a scolding nasal "jhe'jhe'jhe'jhe" to make "pssi'chew! jhe'jhe'jhe'jhe", or a softer, more chattering and more Blue Tit-like "eh'eh'eh'eh". It also uses a monosyllabic "sip" and a high-pitched "tsip'sip" note in territorial disputes. The song is highly variable between individuals, and is a loud and clear ringing series of five to seven notes delivered on an even scale. Versions include "tiiup tiiup tiiup tiiup tiiup", "tue'tue'tue'tue'tue", "tseer'tserr'tseer'tseer'tseer" or a more disyllabic "p'chirh p'chirh p'chirh p'chirh p'chirh p'chirh".

Nuthatch
Sitta europaea

Length: 12–14.5cm
Wingspan: 22.5–27cm

A stocky, short-tailed and 'spear-headed' bird, the Nuthatch is usually seen climbing on vertical trunks and branches and often coming downwards head-first, always rather active and restless as it searches for insects and other food. The bill is long and deep like a small chisel, the upperparts are plain blue-grey, and it has a strong black line through the eye from bill to nape. The throat is whitish, and the remainder of the underparts are rufous-buff, darker and more intensely coloured on the flanks with a rich red-brown vent that is boldly spotted with white. Females are duller and are less deeply coloured below. Juveniles are duller still, and lack the chestnut flanks. Birds of the nominate Scandinavian race are white on the belly, highlighting the chestnut on the vent to maximum effect. It is quite distinctive in flight, travelling in short swooping undulations, not unlike a small woodpecker.

A woodland bird found in deciduous and mixed forest, it favours mature trees, particularly very old gnarled and decaying ones that offer nooks and crannies for feeding and cavities for nesting. In the far north of its range it will nest in pure coniferous forest. It has expanded its range in Britain from strongholds in the south and west into north-western and north-eastern England, and with a small population now established in southern Scotland. It is commonly found in parks and large gardens, and also in mature hedgerows and smaller wooded areas, as long as trees are not too widely spaced. It is a regular visitor to bird feeders and tables, especially where the garden contains, or is adjacent to, large trees, and can be quite aggressive towards other garden birds in this situation. It will also feed readily on the ground, moving with jerky hops. Attention may be drawn to loud tapping sounds, as the bird wedges a nut in a crevice and opens it by hammering with its bill.

Breeding commences in April, and the nest is a hole in a large tree. It uses an existing hole, and will often plaster the entrance with mud to customise the diameter. Inside the cavity the nest is made of bark fibres and dead leaves, the female doing much of the preparation although the male will assist with the plastering. An average of six to eight eggs are laid and incubation is solely by the female, for 16–17 days. The young are tended by both parents and fledge after 24–25 days.

Very vocal, it has a wide variety of rather loud and far-carrying vocalizations that function as territorial, advertising and contact calls. Commonly heard is an excited single or slightly disyllabic "tyupp", "tu'iip" or "twehp", frequently repeated and often in rapid couplets, such as "twehp'twehp, twehp'twehp, twehp'twehp". It also gives a flatter, quick "chud'ud'ud", and a longer "chtd'chtd'chtd'chtd'chtd'chtd" or "thk'thk'thk'thk'thk". It makes a conversational "sit" contact note when feeding generally, and a shivering silvery "fsr'r'r'r'r'r". The song is variable, usually a loud clear piping whistle, repeated either slowly as "viou' viou' viou' viou' viou'…" or "pwee' pwee' pwee' pwee' pwee…", or rapidly as a liquid trilling "pi'pi'pi'pi'pi'.." or "pr'r'r'r'r'r'r…", and also as a nasal "ve've've've've've've".

Treecreeper
Certhia familiaris

Length: 12.5–14cm
Wingspan: 17.5–21cm

A slight bird with a long and slender shape, this is the only one of our passerines to possess a thin decurved bill. It has the distinctive habit of climbing mouse-like up vertical trunks, in search of insects which it picks from crevices in the bark with its fine bill, its feet splayed apart and a long, stiff and 'spiky' tail pressed against the tree as it ascends. It typically begins at the base of a tree and climbs up before flying down to the base of an adjoining tree and starting again. It only climbs upwards, unlike the Nuthatch which can descend head-first, and can be easily overlooked owing to the cryptic plumage of its upperparts, which are essentially bark-coloured, with a complex pattern of brown finely marked with whitish spots and streaks. It is white below, faintly tinged brown on the rear flanks and vent, and with a white supercilium that is strongest behind the eye. The sexes are similar, but closer studies have revealed that females forage primarily on the upper parts of tree trunks, whereas males use the lower parts. Juveniles are similarly plumaged to adults but have buff spotting on the mantle and head, and have a shorter tail to begin with. Treecreepers are most likely to be detected by their calls, or may catch one's eye in early spring, when the males fly in spirals around a tree trunk in pursuit of a female.

The Treecreeper is a resident woodland bird and found in deciduous, mixed and coniferous forest. In Britain it favours broad-leaved woodland, often where quite dense, but also occurs commonly in small marginal patches of trees in farmland, hedges, parks, large gardens and in riverine strips of alder and other species. It requires bark with crevices for feeding, and with decaying wood and loose and flaky bark for nesting and roosting. Introduced North American redwoods and Wellingtonia trees are favourite nesting trees, and they may be used in winter for communal roosting during cold weather. These trees are doubtless favoured due to the ease of excavating a nest or roosting cavity, plus the insulating quality of the soft fibrous bark. Nest boxes are sometimes used, and are a good way to lure Treecreepers into a garden, although being insectivorous they will not use bird feeders. They may join mixed feeding flocks in winter, and are vulnerable to very cold winter weather.

Breeding commences in April or May, and five or six eggs are laid. The nest is in a crevice, often in the narrow space behind a flap of rotting bark, and is built by both sexes of twigs, grass and moss, lined with wool and feathers. The female does all the incubation, for 13–17 days, and upon hatching the chicks are fed by both parents. They fledge after 15–17 days, and although only able to fly weakly they can climb well. Two broods are usual.

The song is a very high-pitched, regularly structured little ditty lasting 2–2.5 seconds, starting with high flat notes, accelerating and descending in tone before a flourish at the end, with the penultimate note being the lowest of the sequence and the final note being higher, as in "tseee, tsee'tsee tsi'sisisisi sisoo'wit". The calls are also very high-pitched, as high as a Goldcrest at 8.5kHz, as in a short and often repeated contact call, "zssii" or "tiih", sometimes with a dipping inflexion such as "tsu'ui", and also a harsher, slightly buzzing "zsih'h'h'h" and a more trilling, high and flat "tsirrrr".

Jay
Garrulus glandarius

Length: 32–35cm

Wingspan: 52–58cm

A common and distinctive bird, the Jay often draws attention to itself with its screeching call or its colourful form flapping over the garden trees. It is fairly large and striking, with a longish tail, rounded head and short bill. The body, head and wing coverts are a light pinkish-brown, with a white rump, throat and vent. The tail is black, which contrasts strongly with the rump, and the flight feathers are blackish with chestnut on the upper tertials and a white patch on the secondaries, which is visible at rest. On the 'shoulder' or primary coverts and inner greater coverts, it has a distinctive bright blue panel vermiculated with black. The eye is pale and staring, the forecrown is streaked black and it has an oblong black moustachial patch.

Present in good numbers throughout our region, it favours both deciduous and coniferous forests, but with a special affinity for oak. It can also be found in parks, large gardens, hedgerows and scattered smaller wooded areas. It is mostly resident, but northern birds often move south, and in autumn they can be seen more widely. A century ago the Jay was in decline, due to persecution by gamekeepers and hunting for its plumage, as the brilliant blue wing feathers were in demand by milliners and for fishing flies. Numbers have now recovered well. They collect

BEING MOBBED BY
GOLDCREST AND COAL TIT

and store acorns as winter food caches, and in autumn can often be seen in flight transporting acorns to their hiding places. Indeed, the Jay is one of the most important natural vectors of acorns, allowing oak trees to spread uphill in particular, and the distribution of several oak species is quite dependent on its presence. Its diet also includes a wide range of invertebrates, including many pest insects, as well as beech mast and other seeds, and fruits such as rowan and blackberries. It will also take young birds, eggs, mice and other small mammals. Jays are often wary, yet may be seen regularly in gardens and will visit bird tables for scraps.

Breeding commences in March or April, and both sexes take part in the building of a deep cup of twigs and stems, mixed with a little earth and lined with fine roots and hair, and placed in the fork of a tree or against a trunk. Both sexes incubate the four or five eggs, which hatch after 18 days. The female broods the small chicks at first while the male brings food to her, then both parents take part in feeding. Fledging occurs after 20–23 days.

The commonly heard vocalization is the harsh and raucous call, a rather hoarse upwards-inflected "skaaaaaak!" or "schaaaaach", often repeated twice or more. It is used as an alarm or warning, such as when mobbing an owl, or as an advertising call. It has a range of other calls, less frequently heard, such as an almost perfect copy of the call of the Common Buzzard, as in "pee'yah", some conversational, gruff "eerhhh" calls, a soft rising "eerrrrr'eh", and other softer mewing notes. It also has a song, often only audible from close range, which is a fairly sweet subdued warbling and twittering, and often includes mimicry. It is usually sung by the male, typically in late winter and early spring, but occasionally at other times of year.

Magpie
Pica pica

Length: 40–51cm (inc. tail of 20–30cm)
Wingspan: 52–60cm

This noisy character is familiar to many, with its distinctively pied plumage and long tail. The tail is glossed green and exceeds the length of the body, and males have longer tails than females. The head, breast, vent and upperparts are black, the belly white, and it has a long white stripe along the scapulars. The wings are black with a blue gloss and a large white panel across the whole of the primaries. The metallic sheen on the wings and tail varies between green, blue and purple, depending on the angle of the light. The flight is rather flappy, fluttering and direct. Juveniles are similar to adults, but sooty-headed, shorter tailed and less glossy.

The Magpie is a common and widespread resident found in a wide range of habitats. They are very adaptable, which has enabled them to colonize many new urban and suburban localities since the 1960s, although apparently this population 'surge' has now stabilized. It generally favours lightly wooded open country, with adequate open ground and short grass for feeding, and can be found in open deciduous and coniferous woodland, farmland with hedges, and often occurs close to man in villages, parks and gardens.

Its diet comprises largely insects (especially beetles), worms and other invertebrates, as well as fruit, seeds, carrion, food scraps and occasionally small vertebrates. It is often seen

MAGPIES AND
STARLINGS SCAVENGING

plundering the nests of small birds of their eggs or young, but generally only does this when feeding its own offspring. In winter Magpies become very gregarious, feeding in flocks of variable size, and also gathering at communal roosts in the evenings. These flocks break up in spring when birds begin their breeding.

Magpie pairs are monogamous, mating for life, and begin breeding each April, when they build a ragged nest of sticks strengthened with mud, lined with softer plant material and with a roughly built dome of twigs over the top. Five or six eggs are laid, and the female incubates for 17–20 days. Both parents take part in feeding the young, which fledge after 26–31 days. A strong trend towards earlier laying has been identified and may be partly explained by recent climate change.

It has a range of calls, all rather harsh and unmusical, with the familiar 'rattle' call frequently heard. It is a "cha" or "jakh" note, rapidly repeated to make a staccato chattering, as in "jakh'akh'akh'akh'akh'akh", and is typically given in alarm or anxiety, such as when mobbing predators. Another commonly heard call is a two-note "ch'chack", "akh'jack" or "schrach-ak", and a single, more drawn-out "shree'akh", which are used in a conversational context and often heard when a group of birds are together. It has other, less well-defined harsh notes, and also a rarely heard song, used in courtship, which is a subdued chuntering and twittering interspersed with some sweet notes.

Jackdaw
Corvus monedula

Length: 30–34cm
Wingspan: 67–74cm

An amiable and gregarious small blackish crow, the Jackdaw is often seen in tight flocks in farmland and frequently mixed with Rooks. At range it can appear all dark, but with a reasonable view it shows a pale light-blue eye and a grey nape and sides to the head, contrasting with the charcoal-grey upperparts and black face, crown and throat. The underparts and remainder of the plumage are dark grey, and it has a rather short and slender bill. The nominate race or 'Nordic' Jackdaw, which breeds in Scandinavia,

NOMINATE RACE

BRITISH RACE

has slightly paler and more mottled underparts, as well as a clearly defined silver collar at the lower edge of the neck sides. Juveniles are duller-plumaged and less contrasting.

Resident throughout our region, although northern birds wander southwards in autumn and winter. It is often found close to man, using chimneys and other cavities in buildings for nesting, and otherwise occurs in many types of open habitat with scattered trees. It often favours deciduous woodland where old hollow or mature trees with cavities are available, such as in old parkland and large gardens, and also occurs in

farmland with mature hedgerows and locally in mountainous or cliff habitats and quarries. It feeds mostly on the ground, but also in trees. Its diet includes insects and other invertebrates, seeds, food scraps, shoreline fish carrion, animal feeds (particularly around outdoor-reared pigs), and it is more likely to take food from bird tables than other *Corvus* species. Jackdaws can often be seen together in pairs, being attentive to each other or flying around in tandem, as the male watches his female to make sure the offspring are all his own!

The nest is made within a large cavity, often in the chimney of a house or in the porous roof of an old building such as a church. It commonly nests in a large hole in a dead tree, and will use nest boxes with a large interior. Breeding commences in March and April, and both sexes take part in building the nest with a variable amount of

twigs, depending on the size of the cavity. Nest territories are very small, so Jackdaws can often live in loose colonies. The female incubates the four or five eggs for 18–20 days, and both sexes feed the young. The fledglings leave the nest after 30–33 days.

A vocal bird, so much so that it is named after its commonly heard call, a rather high, bright and pleasing "tjakk!", "khakk" or "kyak", often repeated in a series or given in chorus by a flock, when it can sound like "k'chak k'chik k'chakk", or an even faster 'yickering' sound, such as when gathering to roost. It gives this or similar calls at varying volumes and intensities, such as quieter conversational 'chakking' from pairs sitting together, or when adults announce their return to the nest. It gives more of a crow-like 'caw' in alarm, a harsh drawn-out "jaairrr" or "kyarrrr". It also has a song, a quiet medley of call notes run together.

Rook
Corvus frugilegus

Length: 41–49cm
Wingspan: 81–99cm

The Rook is an all-black crow with a blue or bluish-purple metallic sheen to its plumage, visible in bright sunlight. The main difference between the Rook and the very similar Carrion Crow is the grey bill, with greyish-white skin around the bill base and extending up to the eye. It lacks the nostril feathering that is so prominent on both the Carrion Crow and Raven, and as a consequence the bill appears more pointed and dagger-like. The head is more domed with a peaked crown, and when walking it often appears fuller-bellied. Juveniles look very similar to Carrion Crows, lacking the adult Rook's whitish face and having black feathering over the nostrils until their first winter.

It is common and widespread across the region, and generally resident, although birds from the north of its range move south- and westwards in autumn and winter. It is essentially a lowland bird, favouring agricultural areas, where it can be found in flocks feeding in pastures and on ploughed fields. It appears to be unaffected by changes in agriculture. As a garden bird it is unlikely to be found within a garden, except in open rural areas, but may frequently be seen flying over or lurking in nearby treetops. Its diet consists of invertebrates, particularly earthworms and insect larvae, which it finds by probing the ground with its strong bill. It also eats cereal grain, acorns, fruit, small mammals such as voles, and the eggs

A ROOKERY

days while the male brings food to her. The chicks are fed by both parents and leave the nest after 32–34 days. The call is a simple 'caw' similar to that of the Carrion Crow, but differs in that it is less rolling and more grinding in quality, a harsher, hoarse and nasal "graaah" or "geeeah", and a multi-syllable "gra'gra' grrahh". This call is lower in pitch than the Carrion's and delivered in a flat and even tone, but it can vary the call somewhat and also makes a higher-pitched 'hiccup' sound, "khuow". Females also give a longer higher-pitched call, as in "kraaa-a". As Rooks are so often in flocks, their calls sound repeated and even overlapping, and when at a rookery can provide a near-deafening cacophony of sound when at close range. The male gives a 'song' in courtship, which is a medley of various call notes, said to resemble the song of the Starling.

of ground-nesting birds. Rooks may also forage on saltmarshes and along the seashore.

Breeding commences in February, when their nests are very noticeable in the leafless treetops. They always nest colonially, and favour areas with tall trees for their rookeries, such as on the edges of woodland, but most commonly in isolated stands of trees and copses in farmland areas and in adjacent villages. The nests may be reused year after year, and are built by both adults of branches and twigs that are broken off trees rather picked up from the ground, although some are likely to be stolen from nearby nests! Usually three to five eggs are laid, and are incubated by the female for 15–17

Carrion Crow & Hooded Crow

Corvus corone &
Corvus cornix

Length: 44–51cm
Wingspan: 93–104cm

CARRION
CROW

The Carrion Crow is the familiar all-black corvid over much of Britain and western Europe, with the similar Hooded Crow replacing it across Ireland, Scotland, Scandinavia and eastern Europe. They are both so similar in morphology and habits that they were considered by most authorities to be just geographical races of one species, as a limited amount of hybridization occurs where ranges overlap. Since 2002, however, the Hooded Crow has been elevated to full species status. The Carrion Crow has a slight metallic sheen to its plumage, but is otherwise uniform in colour.

Similar to the Common Raven, it can told apart by its smaller size, rounded tail, shorter bill, shorter wings and weaker flight, plus clear vocal differences. It is almost impossible to separate from a juvenile Rook, however, but shows a blunter, thicker bill. Generally less gregarious than the Rook, and also a solitary nester, it can however

HOODED
CROW

CARRION CROWS
MOBBING LESSER
BLACK-BACKED GULL

carrion and scraps, and will kill and eat any small animal they can catch. They will also steal eggs and young chicks.

Breeding commences in April, and both species build a ragged nest of sticks and twigs, usually in a tree or bush and bound together with earth and lined with hair and wool. Three or four eggs are laid, and the female incubates for 18–20 days.

Both sexes feed the young, which fledge after 29–30 days. It is not uncommon for a youngster from the previous year's offspring to help rear the new hatchlings. Instead of seeking out a mate, it stays around its parents, looking for food and assisting with the feeding of the new young.

The calls of the Hooded and Carrion Crows are very similar. They are quite vocal, the commonly heard call throughout the year being a repeated, slightly nasal "kraaaah" or a softer "oarrgh", which dip in pitch at the end of the note, with a slightly rolling and liquid tone at times and often repeated in a sequence of 2–6 notes. This call can be of varying pitch, and is sometimes delivered more urgently on a level tone, such as "kraaaa! kraaah!" or "kruaah-kruaah". The female can give a more mechanical-sounding "krrgh krrgh krrgh", reminiscent of a Raven's call but usually accompanied by the main call to avert any confusion. Hoarse and strangled-sounding variants may also be heard sometimes, and a rarely heard song of subdued variable notes is also given.

form flocks, particularly after breeding. The Hooded Crow is a pale dirty-grey on the body, with black wings and a black hood and breast.

Found commonly in a wide variety of habitats, they favour open country with scattered trees, woodland, parks and farmland with hedgerows, but commonly penetrate into urban areas, their only real habitat requirement being for trees in which to nest. Scavengers by nature, they will take advantage of human-inhabited areas in order to feed on the abundant waste. In Britain they can also be found foraging in tidal habitats, such as estuaries, saltmarshes and coastal areas, and Hooded Crows have a liking for bog habitats. They feed on invertebrates and cereal grain,

Starling
Sturnus vulgaris

Length: 19–22cm

Wingspan: 37–42cm

JUVENILES

Most people are familiar with this ubiquitous bird. It has a metallic green and violet sheen to its black plumage, a short tail and pointed triangular wings. In winter it is profusely spotted with buffish-white spots and has a dark bill, but in summer loses most of the pale spotting and appears wholly glossy black. The bill also turns yellow, with a blue-grey bill base in the male and a yellowish-white one in the female. Juveniles are a mousy grey-brown with a pale throat, gradually acquiring white-spotted black feathers during their first winter.

Resident in Britain and western Europe, with large influxes of birds in winter from further north and east, it is common and found in many different habitats, and is particularly attracted to urban areas. In recent years Starling numbers have declined, possibly attributable to pesticides killing the food on which their young depend. It can be found in woodland, farmland, on seashores, and indeed in almost any open country. Outside the breeding season it is highly gregarious, dispersing widely and sometimes forming massive flocks over roosting sites in the evening, providing a spectacular sight and sound. They fly in a tight spherical formation, frequently expanding, contracting and changing shape, seemingly without any leader. Larger roosts can cause problems through guano pollution killing the trees in which they roost. They forage on the ground, taking fruit, seeds and insects, typically amongst short-cropped grass, and can often be seen around (and sometimes on top of) grazing animals. In gardens they voraciously devour any food left out, and are very fond of fat balls. They will readily use nest boxes, provided the entrance hole is large enough.

Breeding commences in April, and unpaired males build a nest in any kind of hole to attract an unpaired female. The males often decorate nests with flowers and fresh greenery, which the female removes when she moves in and rebuilds it. The nest

WINTER
PLUMAGE

an aerial predator is about, and often a good indication of a Sparrowhawk in the area. The song is a rambling, continuous collection of rather strangled and subdued sounds, throaty warbling and musical whistles, many of them high-pitched, including much mimicry and unusual noises, such as a rising "schweee'errrr" and a descending "wheeeeeooooooo" 'bomb-drop' whistle, plus clicking, gurgling and croaking noises, and scrunching sounds like a handful of ball-bearings being rubbed together. Starlings are famous for mimicking mechanical sounds such as telephones and car alarms!

SUMMER
PLUMAGE

is typically constructed of straw, dry grass and twigs, and lined with feathers, wool, leaves and insect-repelling herbs. Four to five eggs are laid and incubated by both sexes for 12–15 days. The young are fed by both sexes and fledge after 19–22 days.

Starlings are very vocal, with a rich repertoire of song and mimicry. Commonly heard calls include a rasping descending "tchaaeerr", often given when taking flight. Other calls include a sharp repeated "kyik" or "kyett", given in alarm when

House Sparrow
Passer domesticus

Length: 14–16cm
Wingspan: 21–25.5cm

In spite of recent declines in some areas, the House Sparrow was still estimated to be Britain's most common garden bird as recently as 2006. It is a stout, large-headed and thick-billed bird, the male having a grey crown with a chestnut brown nape and head sides between crown and cheek, pale grey cheeks and greyish underparts. It has black lores, chin and throat, and a black upper breast that flares out into a broader patch. The mantle is brown and boldly streaked black, with a grey rump in summer. In winter it is duller and browner overall, with a reduced amount of black on the underparts. The female is more demure, grey-brown all over, heavily streaked on the mantle, and with a buff supercilium.

The House Sparrow is commonly found wherever there is human habitation, although in parts of urban Britain there has been a marked decrease in recent years. It ranges from city centres to small villages and particularly farms, and can be found feeding on farmland, especially in grain crops and typically where there are hedgerows

MALE

and other cover to which it can retreat. It generally avoids exposed, open spaces and densely vegetated or forested areas. House Sparrows are gregarious, nesting colonially and and gathering in communal roosts. Between August and October many colonies are abandoned as birds move onto arable land to take advantage of the temporary abundance of grain. Once the flocks break up in October, nesting colonies are reoccupied. They are aggressive birds, tending to dominate seed feeders in gardens and thereby preventing other birds from getting to the food. They adore black sunflower seeds and sunflower hearts, and close scrutiny of sparrows at feeders filled with cheaper mixed seed will reveal that they throw a lot of unwanted seed on the ground, as they try to get to their choice morsel!

They nest in loose colonies of up to 10–20 pairs, and since they do not defend a proper territory, nests can be as little as 20–30cm apart. Nests are located in crevices, holes and under loose roof tiles in buildings or, more traditionally, in a bush or a hole in a sandbank. Breeding commences in May or earlier, with four or five eggs being laid in a hole or crevice, in a cup-shaped (or sometimes a domed) nest built by both sexes, of grass and straw with a feather lining. The female does the majority of the incubation, which only lasts for 11–14 days. The parents share nesting duties equally, and the young are fed on aphids, caterpillars, weevils and grasshoppers, but seed and grain are the most important foods by the time they fledge. Fledging occurs 14–16 days after hatching, and the young

continue to be fed by the parents for 14 days, or by just the male when the female has already started incubating another brood. They have three broods in a year, and occasionally four. Pairs are faithful to each other for life.

A rather uncomplicated set of vocalizations that sound bright and 'chirpy'. Frequently heard is the 'song' of the male, given when advertising to the female from close to the nest, a series of chirps and cheeps slightly varying in pitch, such as "cheerp cheerp chilp chahp chaairp chearp…", or a more liquid "tchlrrp schleeip schlep tchleeip schleeip schlrrp..", etc. Other calls include a more clipped and drier "cheeup" or "chuurp", often repeated and given excitedly by a group, plus a disyllabic conversational "che'chep". It calls in flight with a single "cherp" note or disyllabic "churrip", and in anxiety or excitement gives a harder more rattling "chrr'rr'rr'rr'rr".

FEMALE

Tree Sparrow
Passer montanus

Length: 12.5–14cm
Wingspan: 20–22cm

The Tree Sparrow has recently suffered a massive decline in Britain, but can still be found locally in various parts of the country. In contrast to the House Sparrow, both sexes are similarly plumaged. It is slightly smaller and more compact than that species, and also brighter, with a red-brown crown and white cheeks that are punctuated with a prominent black cheek spot.

The white extends around the neck in an almost complete collar, plus it has black lores, and a black chin and centre to the throat. The mantle is rufous, strongly marked with black streaks, the rump is brown and the unmarked underparts are pale buffy-brown. The first indication of this species in an area is often the calls given by birds in flight.

A widespread resident in our region, although in Britain it has been subject to population fluctuations, even before the dramatic decrease of recent years. The current crash occurred between the late 1970s and the early 1990s, when the population dropped by 87 per cent! The lack of insects (required to feed its young) in the modern agricultural landscape is a likely cause for the decline, along with changes in farming practices, such as the reduction in winter stubble. It can be found in farmland areas with tall hedgerows, woodland edges and scattered

trees, parkland and other open habitats with occasional trees. It is less frequent around human habitation in Britain and Europe, despite being the common 'urban' sparrow across much of Asia. It does occur in gardens, however, either occupying nest boxes or simply visiting bird tables and feeders. It feeds on grasses, weeds and cereals such as barley and wheat, and in the garden will take seed.

It typically nests in a tree hole or a cavity in a building. Tree Sparrows are gregarious at all seasons, and a grove of old trees with a plentiful supply of hollows would be a favoured site for a colony. However, they are very fickle and large colonies may be deserted after just a few years. Breeding commences in April and May, and both sexes build an untidy cup of twigs and grass,

lined with feathers. Five or six eggs are laid, and both sexes incubate for 12–13 days. The young are tended by both sexes and they fledge after 15–18 days. There are usually two or three broods per season.

The calls and 'song' are similar to those of the House Sparrow, with a repeated cheeping and chirping, but the note has a brisker and drier quality to it and is slightly higher-pitched. The song is a simple "tcheep tchirp tcheep tchirp tcheep tchirp…", varying between just one repeated note or alternating between two notes at slightly different pitches. It also has a sweeter and thinner, rather swallowed and ascending "tssu'eet", and in flight has a distinctive hard and dry "chek", repeated as "chekk-et'et'ett", which becomes a rolling chatter when given by a flock.

Chaffinch
Fringilla coelebs

Length: 14–16cm
Wingspan: 24.5–28.5cm

FEMALE

The Chaffinch is a very common bird across the region and is found in a variety of habitats, as well as being a common sight in many gardens. The male in particular is one of the more handsome members of the garden avifauna, and his bright and cheery song makes for a happy backdrop of sound. Indeed, it is very satisfying to hear the first songsters rattling away merrily at the end of the long winter months. It is rather long-tailed, compact and sparrow-sized, although slimmer and more elegant than a House Sparrow. The male is ruddy-pink from the throat and cheeks down to the belly, with a blue-grey crown, nape and shoulder, a chestnut-brown back and black wings boldly marked with double white wingbars, a plumage which is brightest in spring, with colours duller and more subdued in winter. In all plumages it shows white or pale wingbars, white sides to the tail and a grey-green rump, features that are important for identification in the female particularly. She is much more demure, often looking nondescript, with a sepia-monochrome plumage, dull buffish-white underparts, a pale head and face, and a darker grey-brown crown and nape.

FEMALE

MALE

MALE

well as feeding on seed put out on open ground, but they always prefer a clear view of their surroundings and of any possible dangers. Although generally seed-eating, they will occasionally use peanut feeders. In Britain, breeding commences in April and May, with the nest located in a tree or tall bush. The female makes a neat deep cup of moss, lichen, grass and roots, bound together with spider webs and lined with feathers, with this construction usually built tightly into a branch fork. The female lays four or five eggs, and will do all the incubation, which lasts for 12–13 days. The nestlings are fed by both parents and leave the nest after 13–16 days.

It has a wide repertoire of calls, the most familiar one being a sharp repeated "pink" or "fink", a rather soft "hyupp", frequently heard from flying birds, a clear, upwards-inflected "hweet", and a short buzzing even-toned "hwwrrr" or "zhwrrr" note, rather reminiscent of the song of the Brambling. The Chaffinch's song is one of the more familiar sounds of spring, a loud, vigorous and slightly accelerating series of sweet but hard notes, descending in four tonal steps and ending in a trisyllabic flourish. It is usually unvarying in delivery and can sound almost rattle like, such as "chich-ich-ich-ich-ich-ich churr'rr'rr'rr'rr' cho'cho'cho'cho'cho chippit' churri'weeoo". It typically lasts 2.5–3 seconds, however variations are possible and it may sing with varying and out-of-sequence pitches. The song can be heard from February to July, and less frequently in the autumn.

The Chaffinch is one of the commonest birds in Britain, where it is resident, although numbers are supplemented in winter by migrants from northern Europe. It can be found in a variety of wooded habitats, both coniferous and deciduous, and these can include parks, orchards, gardens and farmland with hedgerows. During the winter months it also ranges onto arable fields and other open areas, usually adjacent to woodland, and where it can often be encountered in flocks mixed with other species. It is commonly found feeding on the ground, retreating to nearby trees when disturbed, only to drop down once more when the coast is clear. In a garden environment Chaffinches frequently use seed feeders and bird tables, as

Brambling
Fringilla montifringilla

Length: 14–16cm
Wingspan: 25–26cm

FEMALE
WINTER
PLUMAGE

The male in summer has a very striking colour scheme, with a glossy blue-black head and mantle offset by a tangerine-orange breast and shoulder. In Britain it is most often seen in the less eye-catching winter dress, but in all plumages the wing is strongly patterned with black and orangey-buff (black with white bars in the summer male), plus a whitish belly neatly spotted with dark on the flanks, a forked blackish tail and a long white central stripe on the rump that is plainly visible in flight. In winter the bill is yellowish with a dusky tip, and the black head and mantle of the male is frosted with pale and brownish fringes. The female has a paler, greyer head with some blackish markings on the crown and a double dark line on the nape, plus an orange band across the upper breast from shoulder to shoulder. They can often be quite unobtrusive when feeding in trees, their presence betrayed only by their nasal calls.

SMALL FLOCK
FEEDING WITH
CHAFFINCH

MALE
SPRING

A Scandinavian breeder that winters throughout Britain and western Europe, its numbers fluctuate from year to year, depending on food availability. In winter it is strongly tied to open woodland and woodland edge, churchyards, large parks and occasionally gardens, particularly where beech mast has fallen, as well as to farmland and fields with hedgerows and scattered trees. It breeds in northern birch forests, mixed and coniferous open woodland, and often in uplands. It regularly visits gardens, often in the company of Chaffinches, taking seed from feeders or bird tables, or may be heard flying over, particularly during autumn influxes. Bramblings may act rather nervously, retreating to treetops before dropping to the ground to feed when there is no disturbance.

It has bred in Britain on a number of occasions, but this is very unusual. Breeding normally commences in May (later if in the far north) and the female builds a bulky cup of moss and grass similar to that of the Chaffinch, bound with spider webs, camouflaged with lichen and bark and lined with feathers, hair and down. It is frequently built in a birch tree, and five to seven eggs are laid. The female incubates for 11–12 days and both sexes take part in feeding the young, which fledge after 13–14 days.

The commonly heard call is a twangy, slightly explosive and sharply ascending nasal "dweee'ap", "chwa'ingt" or "thwaai'ip", given both in flight and when perched. It also has a Crossbill-like "chup chup" or "chyk chyk", given in flight, harder, deeper and more nasal than that of the Chaffinch. The song is a simple monosyllabic note, a fairly long, low drawn-out nasal buzz or wheeze, such as "nwhhaaeerrrr"or "zhwheeeehhh", lasting about 0.6–0.8 seconds and repeated persistently and monotonously, at regular intervals several seconds apart. It may also add a liquid buzzy note, shorter and lower than the song buzz, and a quicker higher-pitched version with a sparrow-like quality, given more excitedly. The anxiety note is a repeated short, high-pitched penetrating "tzilt" or "zrriillt".

Greenfinch
Carduelis chloris

Length: 14–16cm
Wingspan: 24.5–27.5cm

A common and familiar garden bird, often seen sitting prominently and singing, or engaging in bat-like display flights over the rooftops. It is a big-headed, plump and compact finch, readily recognized by the bright yellow wing panel formed by yellow edging to the primaries, plus a deep, thick whitish or pale pink bill. It also shows prominent blocks of yellow on the sides of the tail, which contrast with the remainder of the black tail and are most noticeable when seen in flight. The male is uniform light green, with a more yellow tone on the breast, and a brighter yellow-green rump. The upperparts are rather greyer, with a grey panel on the wing and grey head sides. The female is duller, brownish-green and faintly streaked on the mantle, and juveniles are brown and more streaked, with paler underparts.

A common resident in our region, with some immigration in winter by northern birds. A bird of the woodland edge, it favours taller trees in clearings, scrub, hedgerows, parks and gardens, but can also be found on arable fields and other open habitats, often feeding on the ground. The Greenfinch has become a very widespread and common feeder in gardens and this has probably insulated it against potential losses due to agricultural intensification. Its diet consists of large seeds, such as rose hips and cereal grain, and sunflower seeds are a particular favourite. Invertebrates such as insects are also taken, particularly for feeding to nestlings. Greenfinches regularly visit bird tables, and particularly seed feeders, favouring those with a small perch so that they can sit facing the feeder. Like House Sparrows, they are quite fussy about which seeds they eat, and where mixed seed is used they will often throw all the other seeds onto the ground so as to get to the black sunflower seeds. They can also be attracted to peanuts and fat balls, and will eat fruit where available.

Breeding commences in April or May, and the female builds a bulky cup of grasses, stems and moss, lined with hair, fine stems and feathers, the male accompanying her as she does so. The nest is usually in a bush or hedge, with four or five eggs laid and incubated by the female only, for 14–15 days. Both parents feed the nestlings a regurgitated mix, and the young fledge after 14–16 days. Greenfinches have two or three broods per season, and the female may lay again soon after the previous brood has fledged, leaving the male to feed the young while she incubates a new clutch.

A vocal bird, with a range of bright and bouncy calls. Typically heard are monosyllabic 'chips' and nasal

FEMALE

MALE

MALE

sounds, such as an upward-slurred "ju'wee" and higher-pitched "chwai'ii" or "pwai'ii" notes, which may act as alarm or anxiety notes. It also gives a single or repeated "chud", "jup" or "ju'jup",

often given in flight, or extended into a slow trilling "chid'id'id'id'id'id'id" or "jup'up'up'up'up", plus a faster, more silvery trilling "tchrr'r'r'r'r'r'r'r". It has two song types: the first is a frequently heard, very nasal, drawn-out and downwards-inflected "djeeeeeuuuooo", lasting 1–1.6 seconds in length, with regular longer pauses between.

A flatter or slightly upwards-inflected version of this is also given, as in "jweeeiiie". The more complex song incorporates many of these calls, including the "djeeuuuoo" sound, and alternates between Canary-like trills and other more slowly delivered notes, such as "djuw djuw djuw, jup jup jup, chi'di'di'di'di'dit, ju'wee, chud'chd'chd, chid'id'id 'id'id'id'id, ju'wee, djui djui djui djui, tilng tilng tilng tilng, tiisssrrrrrr, djeeeeeuuuooo…", etc. The song is often given in a bat-like display flight.

Goldfinch
Carduelis carduelis

Length: 12–13.5cm

Wingspan: 21–25.5cm

The Goldfinch is one of the most attractive birds likely to be seen in a garden. The head is white with a large red patch from the forehead around the face to the chin, and with a black crown and nape that curls downwards and forwards to the shoulder. The wings are black with a broad golden-yellow stripe across the flight feathers and greater coverts, and large white spots on the tips of the flight feathers, visible at rest. The underparts are white with buffy-brown flanks and

JUVENILE

an incomplete breast band. The mantle is brown, the rump is white and the forked tail is black with white spots. The sexes are rather similar, but on closer inspection males can be distinguished by a larger, darker red mask that extends just behind the eye; in females the mask falls short of the eye. The bill is long and pointed, ideal for teasing out small seeds. Juveniles are similar to adults except for having a plain head, a greyer back, and a brown-streaked breast. The collective noun for a group of Goldfinches is, appropriately enough, a 'charm'. Their population underwent a serious decline in the 1970s and 80s, probably as a result of the shift towards intensive agriculture, but they now seem to be thriving, particularly in and around gardens.

Resident across most of Britain and the Continent, although more easterly and northern populations move south in winter, outside the breeding season it can often be seen in flocks, feeding on weedy margins. It favours deciduous and mixed woodland edges, farmland hedgerows, orchards, parks, gardens and overgrown waste ground, frequently close to human habitation. The favoured diet consists of small seeds from plants such as thistles, teasels, daisies, dandelion, alder and birch, with the seeds often eaten when only half-ripe. Insects and other invertebrates are taken in summer, and especially for feeding nestlings. Goldfinches increasingly use garden bird feeders, favouring sunflower hearts, black sunflower seeds and peanuts, but most popular of all are nyger seeds, which can be provided for them in special nyger seed feeders. These are similar to a normal seed feeder but have very small holes,which prevent the tiny seeds from spilling out and also allow access only to thin-billed birds such as Goldfinches.

Breeding commences in April and May, and the female builds a cup-shaped nest of moss, grass and lichen, lined with wool and plant down. The nest is usually in a tree towards the end of a spreading branch, and four to six eggs are laid. Incubation is by the female for 13–15 days, and both parents feed the young until fledging takes place at 14–17 days. The young are dependent on the adults for at least one week after leaving the nest. There are two, and sometimes three, broods in a season.

A vocal bird with a variety of calls, the typical contact call being a cheery, variable "twiddit'widdit", also given in single "twtt" components or extended into "di'wit'iwit'iwidli'wit", when it sounds more like a segment of song. It also gives a slightly mewing and nasal "tch'weeoo", "theoo'wt" and "diu'lii", and a harsh buzzing "jhr'r'r'r'r'r" or "jjh'jjh'jjh'jit". The song, given from a perch and also in flight, is a bright, fast, tinkling, rattling and trilling sequence with a bell-like quality, as in "twiddli'widdli'twidi'trrrwiddit-ti'r'r'r'r'r'r'r'r-jjeeoow", sometimes given in a continuous sequence or in well-marked phrases of 2–3 seconds long, interspersed with pauses. Although quite complex and often variable, it is usually recognizable by the inclusion of call notes.

MALE

Siskin
Carduelis spinus

Length: 11–12.5cm
Wingspan: 20–23cm

MALE

The Siskin is superficially similar in colour to the Greenfinch, but is smaller, brighter and more delicate. It has a thinner, pointed bill, and at all ages shows yellow bases to the outer tail feathers. The male has a black crown, lores and chin, with a lemony greenish-yellow face, eyebrow, breast and rump. The mantle is green with narrow black streaks, and the wings are black with boldly contrasting yellow wingbars on the greater coverts and shoulder. The belly is white, with black streaking on the flanks. Females are duller and lack the stronger yellow tones, and are dull green on the head, greenish-white on the rump and white below. Juveniles are paler and very streaky. Siskins can be quite acrobatic when feeding, hanging upside down in the manner of a Blue Tit.

A resident over much of central and eastern Europe and southern Scandinavia, in Britain it is largely concentrated in the north and west, occurring more locally further south and east. In winter, immigrants from the northern and eastern regions swell the resident population, and at this season it is commonly found in birch and alder stands along watercourses, as well as in parks and gardens. It frequently gathers in large mixed winter flocks with other seed-eaters, such as Lesser Redpolls. In the breeding season it favours mixed and coniferous forest, with a special preference for spruce. Formerly much more localized in Britain, in recent decades it has expanded its range greatly with the increase in commercial conifer plantations. Like the Goldfinch, it has a narrow pointed bill and this is reflected in its diet,

FEMALE

MALE AND FEMALE AT A FEEDER

frequently. It also utters a simple "tchiou", and commonly gives a chittering dry trill "cht't't't't't't", uttered conversationally when feeding with other birds or flying together. The song is a rapid, undulating collection of trilling, twittering and repeated call notes, sometimes including a strangled and drawn-out, high nasal wheeze "jhwrrrrrr" near the end of the sequence, as in "dwee'dwee'dwee chich'ich'ich'ich, tsirri tsirri pi'tiou pi'tiou pi'tiou cht't't't't't't't ch'wee ch'wee jhwrrrrrr djiew djiew…", etc.

which mainly comprises cone seeds such as birch, alder, spruce and pine, although in the breeding season it will also eat invertebrates. Siskins visit gardens when food is hard to find in their natural habitats, and seem to be especially attracted to red-coloured feeders! They will take peanuts, fat and seeds, particularly nyger and sunflower.

Conifer trees are preferred for nesting, with both sexes building a cup of grass and moss, lined with roots, hair and wool, and located towards the end of a branch. Breeding commences in April, and four or five eggs are laid. Incubation is solely by the female, for 12–13 days, and the young are fed by both parents with a regurgitated gruel. They fledge after 13–15 days. Siskins commonly have two or even three broods, with the male often taking care of the fledged young while the female begins incubating the next clutch.

Typical call notes heard from flying birds include a downwards-inflected, dissyllabic "b'diow" and an upwards-inflected "dju'lii", "b'deee" or "diu'lee", both given equally

MALE

Linnet
Carduelis cannabina

Length: 12.5–14cm

Wingspan: 21–25.5cm

The Linnet is a familiar bird of open country, although less inclined to reach gardens in a more urban setting. It is a small and slim finch, with a longish cleft tail with whitish feather edges, and whitish edges to the primaries that show at rest and in flight. The male is rather colourful, with a grey head and nape and a red patch on the forehead, and a large crimson breast patch that is variable in intensity with wear. The throat is whitish, mottled and streaked grey, the belly is white, and both sexes show a brown mantle. Females are rather duller, having a grey-brown head with a paler patch on the cheek and a buff streaky breast. Juveniles are duller still, with more pronounced streaking. A gregarious bird, it often forms flocks outside the breeding season, and in common with many of its relatives has a rapid and gently undulating flight.

A resident across Britain and western Europe, but a summer visitor only in Scandinavia. In the breeding season it can be found in open country with thick bushes, such as on farmland, in scrub, hedgerows, thickets, industrial wastelands and parks with rank weedy growths, and particularly on heaths, where it shows a special preference for gorse. Outside the breeding season it ranges more widely onto open fields, saltmarshes and dune slacks, and frequently occurs on rough open ground with a plentiful supply of seed-bearing plants. It is not a natural garden bird, and unlikely to visit feeding stations, but an unkempt weedy rural or suburban garden may attract Linnets. They require small- to medium-sized weed seeds, and have suffered in recent decades with the intensification of modern farming and the increased use of herbicides.

MALE
SUMMER
PLUMAGE

FEMALE

Often given in flight and especially on take-off, the call is a rapid, staccato but bright "chud'ut'ut" or a "chd'it chd'it". It also gives a nasal twanging "chi'ou", as well as other nasal monosyllabic notes sounding more like short segments of song. The advertising song of the male is a varied ensemble of twittering, trills and nasal fluty sounds, run together in a rambling, often rather low-key sequence, and frequently just with short segments repeated idly. In full voice, however, it can give a continuous collection of notes that span a wide frequency range, such as "chippeti-chippeti jiou chp't-chp't-chp't pt'idoo dzhrrrr seee'oo chiwee chu'chu'chu' trr'r'r'r'r chi'oo" and "chi' whii'whii pt'pee'tiou ch'ch'ch'wheeea bt'bt'bt'piouu", "chrr'r'r'r'chee'chee'chee' ch'wrrrr tu'wee tu'wu ti'wheeeoo".

Linnet numbers in Britain declined by 41 per cent during 1972–96, although populations have since stabilized, possibly as a result of the expansion of oilseed rape, the seeds of which they relish. The bird's scientific name is derived from its fondness for hemp.

Breeding commences in April and May, and the female builds the nest. A cup of grass, moss and twigs, lined with hair and wool, it is placed inside a bush. Four to five eggs are laid, and incubated by the female for 13–14 days. Both sexes take part in feeding the young, which are fed on seeds and leave the nest after 13–14 days.

FEMALE

Lesser Redpoll
Carduelis cabaret

Length: 11.5–14cm
Wingspan: 20–22.5cm

The Lesser Redpoll is a small, rather dark little finch, with a short, stubby yellowish bill. It has a small red patch on the forehead, and black on the lores and chin. The upperparts are brown, streaked darker brown on the crown, nape and mantle. The underparts are buffish, whiter on the belly with brown streaks on the shoulder and down the flanks, plus dark streaks on white undertail coverts. The male has a variable amount of pinky-red on the throat, breast and rump, brightest in spring, when the female can also show a rosy hue on the breast. The wing is dark with a buffy wingbar formed by paler tips to the greater coverts, matching the other buff areas of its general coloration. The similar Common or 'Mealy' Redpoll is paler and greyer, lacking the buffy tones, and with a white wingbar.

The Lesser Redpoll is mostly resident in Britain, southern Scandinavia and central Europe, usually wintering within its breeding range although dispersing after nesting, with some British birds known to move south. It can be found in mixed and coniferous woodlands, with a special preference for the latter, and also in birch, alder, willow, scrubby areas and hedgerows. In winter it particularly favours alder and birch trees along watercourses, where it can often be found feeding along with Siskins and Goldfinches. The Common or 'Mealy' Redpoll of Scandinavia is a winter visitor to Britain in small numbers. Redpolls feed on very small seeds, such as those of alder, spruce and birch, usually foraging among small branches where they are quite agile and acrobatic as they hang upside down. During the breeding season they also feed on insects. They are occasional visitors to gardens in the winter months, feeding on the ground on fallen seeds or at bird tables and feeders, where they will

eat sunflower hearts and nyger seeds. Gardens with birch or alder trees can attract them, along with Siskins.

Breeding commences in May, and sometimes several pairs of birds will nest close together in a loose colony. The female builds an untidy cup-shaped nest in a shrub or tree; the nest will be made of fine twigs, grass and stems, and lined with down, feathers and hair. Four or five eggs are laid, and the female incubates them for 12 days. The young are fed by both parents and fledge after 14–15 days. They are often double-brooded.

The typical call, often heard in flight, is a dry rattling "che'che'che'che", and it also gives a higher and sweeter, more slowly repeated "chie'chie'chie". It also has a typical *Carduelis* call, a nasal rising "chwaiii" or "djuu'wi", and a longer rolling buzzing note "dzhiiiiiirrrrrr", given either singly or included in the more developed song. The song is a rather unhurried, staccato and unmusical collection of call notes delivered in roving flights and also from a perch, as in "chi'chi'chi tzrrrrrrrrr chi'chi' dweeeeiiii tway'tway'tway' dweeeiii che'che'che dzhiiiiirr che'che'che' di'di'di tway'tway'tway' dzhiiiirrr che'che'che'…", etc.

Common Crossbill

Loxia curvirostra

Length: 15–17cm
Wingspan: 27–30.5cm

MALE

A stocky finch, comparable to the Greenfinch in build and with a thick neck and large head. The bill has elongated tips to the mandibles, which cross over, an adaptation for prising seeds out of conifer cones. The tail is rather short and deeply cleft, visible in the undulating flight. Males are red all over except for dark brown wings and tail and a pale vent. Females are grey-green, diffusely streaked on the mantle and with a greenish yellow rump. Young birds are grey-brown and streaked all over. Attention is usually drawn to this fascinating bird by its characteristic flight call.

Crossbills are nomadic, highly irruptive and able to travel long distances when new food sources are required. They are specialists at feeding on conifer cones, extracting the seeds

FEMALE

MALE

FEMALE

with their unique bills, and are most likely to occur where pine and spruce are found. In Britain they are found in scattered pockets of suitable habitat, such as in upland areas of Scotland and Wales, as well as in the conifer-forested areas of England, where their range has spread with the increase in commercial conifer plantations. During irruptions they can occur much more widely, with small vocal flocks flying along the coasts and dispersing inland, always in search of fresh conifer cones. At this time they are most likely to occur in or over gardens, especially where suitable conifer habitat is found. They have a liking for water, and so may appear at birdbaths or ponds in order to drink and bathe.

Breeding can occur at any time of year, even sometimes in the depths of winter, depending on the availability of food. Nestlings can even reduce their metabolic rate in order to cope with cold weather. The nest is usually on the side branch of a conifer, and built of grass, moss and wool, on a bed of twigs. Three to five eggs are laid, and

the female incubates for 14–15 days, sitting tight while the male brings her food. The young are fed by both adults, and fledge after 20–25 days, but remain dependent on their parents for a further three or four weeks.

Often vocal, with the calls dividing into those given in flight and in excitement. The 'flight' call (not necessarily given in flight, however) is a fairly loud and explosive repeated "glipp glipp.." or "chlip chlip chlip". The 'excitement' call is a deeper, highly infectious call, repeated excitedly, and can be described as "chuop, choup…" or "chuk, chuk...". A downwards-inflected "tchi'choo tchi'choo" call is also given. The song is a fairly slow collection of call notes, whistles and nasal trills, interspersed with some higher "chiree chiree" sounds, such as "chiree chiree chiree chup-chup-chup chue cheu cheu dzhirrroo dzhirrroo chip chip chiree chiree tup tup tup….", etc. Recent studies have shown that there are as many as seven different 'cryptic' forms of Common Crossbill occurring in north-western Europe, all with subtly different calls.

Bullfinch
Pyrrhula pyrrhula

Length: 15.5–17.5cm
Wingspan: 22–29cm

One of the most exotic-looking and attractive birds likely to be encountered in a garden, the Bullfinch has a plump and rounded body, a large head and a short, thick black bill. A black cap extends on to the face and around the bill, with a black tail contrasting with the white rump and black wings, plus a broad whitish wingbar on the tips of the greater coverts. The upperparts are grey, tinged browner in the female. The male has soft pinkish-red underparts from cheek to belly; on the female these are greyish-buff. Bullfinches are usually encountered sneaking along hedgerows, their white rumps a sure indicator as they flit discreetly from bush to bush, with their call often being the first indication of their presence. The nominate race or 'Northern Bullfinch', which occasionally occurs in Britain as a winter visitor, is larger than the resident British race, and the underparts of the male are a more intense rosy-pink, while the upperparts are paler.

Generally rather secretive, the Bullfinch favours deciduous and mixed woodland with dense undergrowth, as well as coniferous forest in the north of its range. It can be found along woodland edge, clearings, tall scrub, hedgerows, parks, large gardens, churchyards and seasonally in orchards.

FEMALE

MALE

MALE

It is resident in Britain, but has undergone a sharp fall in numbers in recent decades, with the loss of choice hedgerow and woodland edge habitat and the general intensification of agriculture. This decline followed a sharp increase in the 1950s, when Bullfinches caused problems to the fruit-growing industry, leading to widespread trapping in order to control their numbers. Their diet consists of the seeds of fleshy fruits such as cherries, and the buds of fruit trees. They also eat insects and feed their nestlings on invertebrates. In a garden they will also take seed from a hanging seed feeder, being particularly fond of sunflower hearts, and will also take suet cake.

Breeding commences in April or May, the female building a nest of twigs, moss and lichen, with a neat inner cup of roots and hair and located in a dense bush. Four to five eggs are laid and incubated solely by the female for 14–16 days, the male bringing food to her as she does so. The young are fed by both parents, the female sitting tight and brooding the hatchlings at first while the male brings food. The young fledge after

15–17 days, and there are usually two broods. Unlike many other garden birds, breeding pairs of Bullfinch stay together throughout the year rather than separating after breeding.

The commonly heard call note is a piping single note, used as a contact call. It is a pleasant soft "peuw" or "heouw", slightly descending at the end and repeated at regular intervals. It can be quite far-carrying. Birds of the nominate race or 'Northern Bullfinch' have a different 'trumpeting' call, a higher-pitched "heeh" or "pihh", as well as a quiet "tip" note. The song, usually given by the male, is rarely heard, no doubt partly due to its being rather quiet and often only audible from close range. It is a rambling twittering without clear phrases, including typical call notes and some very nasal and deep double notes similar to the call, as well as long purring wheezes and higher-pitched long piping notes, such as "hong-hong tu'tu'tu'didi'peew heeuuuw pwrrrrrr heeeeee hong-hong tu'di'tu'di'tuu hwrrrrrr…".

FEMALE

Hawfinch
Coccothraustes coccothraustes

Length: 16.5–18cm
Wingspan: 29–33cm

A Starling-sized finch with a massive bill, capable of cracking any nuts or fruit stones that cross its path! The mandibles and jaw muscles are so powerful that they can crush cherry stones by exerting a pressure of 10.5kg per square cm, in order to reach the cherry seed inside. Hawfinches have a distinctive outline, with a short tail, large head and bill, and are often seen in a bounding flight, when the broad white band on the tail tips and bold white band on the primaries are both displayed. The overall coloration is buff and brown, with an

FEMALE

MALE
SUMMER
PLUMAGE

orangey-buff head, a black line from eye to bill and a broad black chin framing the swollen bill, which is grey in summer and yellow-brown in winter. There is a grey 'shawl' around the nape, the mantle is dark chestnut-brown, and the rump is orange-brown. The underparts are pinkish-brown, with a white vent. The closed wing shows a large white patch on the greater coverts and blackish flight feathers. Despite this colourful plumage, they can be very cryptic when feeding on the ground or perched in trees, and are most likely to be located by their sharp little call.

Resident and widespread across the region, although rather localized in Britain and often overlooked owing to its shy nature. It favours mixed and deciduous woodland, with a particular affinity for hornbeam, mature oak, beech and wild cherry, spending much of the time in the very top branches of tall trees. It also frequents other large deciduous tree species, and can be found in riverine belts of trees, avenues, churchyards, parks and large gardens. It is most likely to be encountered in a large suburban or rural garden, particularly if hornbeams are present, and is likeliest in winter when it spreads more widely and immigrant birds arrive in Britain from the Continent. It is not averse to feeding on the ground, where it will take fallen tree seeds. Their diet consists of large hard seeds, buds and shoots, and in summer they will eat invertebrates, especially caterpillars. In England it is most likely to be seen in the south-east, but the population has fallen by an estimated 40 per cent in the past decade and they are nowhere common.

Hawfinches spend the summer in dense tree foliage, with several pairs often nesting close together, and have the unexplained habit of breeding in the same locality before disappearing, only to return a few years later. Breeding commences in April and May, and the nest is a rather flimsy, saucer-shaped platform of twigs, grass and roots, often located in a fork far along the branch of a large deciduous tree. It is built by the female with assistance of the male, with four or five eggs being laid and incubated mostly by the female for 11–13 days. At this stage they are very sensitive and likely to desert the nest if disturbed. The young are fed by both parents and fledge after 12–13 days.

It has a rather limited vocabulary, but the most frequently heard call is a sharp metallic "zzic" or "pix", not dissimilar to the 'tic' call of the Robin and given from a perch or often when in flight. Another more discreet call is an inconspicuous high "zree" or "zseeh", harder to hear in a woodland noisy with birdsong. The song is simple and primitive, a rather quiet series of alternating "zzic" and "sii" notes, given slowly and methodically. It also has a rarely heard, low and quiet whistling "deek-deek tur-wee-wee" or "teek-wa'ree-ree-ree", with a strained quality and often with a liquid and musical end to the phrase reminiscent of the Goldfinch.

GROUP
FEEDING

Yellowhammer
Emberiza citrinella

Length: 15.5–17cm

Wingspan: 23–29.5cm

This colourful bunting is another attractive addition to the garden avifauna, and most likely to be seen in the winter and early spring in large gardens close to suitable habitat. The male is bright yellow on the head and underparts, highlighted with a few dark markings on the head, a rusty-brown wash on the breast and streaks down the flanks. The upperparts are rich brown streaked with black, and in all plumages it shows a rich red-brown rump and uppertail, with white outer feathers on a longish tail that show well in flight. In winter the male is duller, with less yellow on the head and more streaky overall. The female is less colourful, washed with a paler yellow on the head, throat and underparts, and is more streaky overall with a darker crown and cheeks.

A common resident, with some northern birds moving into our region in winter. In Britain it has undergone a sharp decline in recent decades, most probably a result of modern farming practices such as the autumn sowing of crops and the loss of winter stubble. It is typically found in lowland arable and mixed farmland with hedgerows, woodland edge, open bushy country, heaths, wooded pastures and shrubby hillsides. In winter it can often be found in flocks in stubble fields and other open areas. Their diet consists of grass seeds and cereal grain, and in the summer months they eat invertebrates. They are most likely to be attracted into a garden by corn and seed, often in the company of other seed-eaters during the winter, when food shortages in the surrounding countryside are at their most acute.

Breeding commences in May, the female building a nest on or near the ground at the foot of a hedge or in long herbage beneath a

MALE
SINGING

trilling sound, as well as a more liquid "trrp-trrp" when flying together in a flock. The alarm note is a thin "see". The song is familiar to many, and in Britain is traditionally rendered as 'a-little-bit-of-bread-and-no-cheese', which although not entirely accurate, was popularized by Enid Blyton in her children's novels! In reality it is a simple rattling repetition of a single note, repeated 10–15 times, accelerating and rising slightly in both pitch and volume, and finished off with a higher drawn-out terminal note, as in "dji'dji'dji'dji'dji'd ji'dji'dji'dji – shjeeee". The song phrase lasts for 1.8–2.5 seconds, and is often followed by a high descending "tseeoo". Variations occur, and songsters may regularly leave off the terminal "shjeeee" note.

hedge. They will wait for a hedge to come into leaf before building. The nest is made of grass, straw and moss, and three or four eggs are laid, patterned with the fine scribble-like markings so characteristic of buntings. Incubation is chiefly by the female, and lasts for 13–14 days. Both parents feed the young on insects, until fledging after 13–16 days. They often have two or more broods.

The typical contact call note is a dry and rather harsh, slightly downwards-inflected "djou", or a similar even-toned "djih". Dry clicking notes are also given, often in flight or when disturbed, as in "tit'tit'tit tic'atic", sometimes accelerated into a

FEMALE

Reed Bunting
Emberiza schoeniclus

Length: 13.5–15.5cm
Wingspan: 21–28cm

The Reed Bunting is a handsome but occasional visitor to gardens. The male is rather striking, with a black throat outlined by white submoustachial stripes, and a black head with a complete white collar. The blacks become more solid through wear, while in freshly moulted autumn plumage the pale tips to the feathers make the head look browner and the throat is scaled white. Both sexes have warm brown upperparts streaked and patterned with black, with chestnut-brown fringes to the wing feathers. The female is rather more demure and sparrow-like, with a brown crown, dull brown cheeks, and a pale supercilium and eye-ring. The underparts are buffish-white streaked black, densest on the breast where they form a vague diamond of

MALE
SINGING

darker markings. At all ages it has bold white outer tail feathers, visible both in flight and when perched, as the wings and tail are flicked nervously.

A common resident in our region, its numbers are augmented in winter by migrants from further north and east. It favours damp areas with scrub,

WINTER
MALE

FEMALE

bushes and tall herbage, typically in reedbeds and also in marshes, lake margins, bogs, marshy tundra, wet meadows and saltmarshes. It also occurs in drier non-marshy areas some distance from water, and is not infrequently found in arable crops such as barley and rape. Outside the breeding season it ranges more widely, moving onto farmland, stubble fields and grasslands, and occasionally into gardens, where birds will take seed from the ground. They are most likely to be seen in gardens during hard weather or if there is suitable habitat nearby. Their diet consists primarily of seeds, although in the breeding season they will take invertebrates, particularly for their nestlings.

Breeding commences in April and May, and the female builds a cup-shaped nest of grass and moss, lined with finer, softer material. It is usually located on or close to the ground in a hidden place, although occasionally higher up. She lays four or five eggs, and does most of the incubation, which lasts for 12–14 days. The young are fed by both parents and fledge after 12–14 days. Two broods

are typical. Apparently over 50 per cent of Reed Bunting chicks are not fathered by the pair male but are rather the result of an adulterous liaison, the highest recorded rate of any bird!

The commonly heard call is a downwards-inflected, rather penetrating "tseeou" or "zseeo", given as both a contact call and an anxiety call. It also has a nasal rasping "djuh", often uttered by autumn migrants, and a "tzi'tzi", given on the breeding grounds and similar to the Meadow Pipit alarm note. Two variants of song are used by the male, with further variation between individuals. Unpaired males sing a faster, bright and chirpy series of simple rather metallic notes, with 10–12 notes in a sequence lasting 1.5–2 seconds in length, as in "tjew, tjew, tjew tsitsi'zeuw chichi'zree'e'e" or "dze tchew'tchew dze'chichi zweee", whereas once they are paired they sing a slower, halting, and barely musical version, with longer pauses (0.5–1 second) between notes, such as "dzi.. dziwi'.. tzhur'r'r.. tzhur'r'r.. zeuup" or "tju.. tju.. dzing.. dzing.. ji'ji'ji zwee".

Water Rail *Rallus aquaticus*
Length: 23–28cm
Wingspan: 38–45cm

Generally very furtive, the Water Rail is most likely to be seen foraging along the muddy edges of reedbeds. It is a slender bird, with long red legs, a long neck and a long red-and-black bill. The face, neck, breast and belly are a dark blue-grey, and the flanks are boldly marked with black-and-white vertical stripes. The upperparts are dark olive-brown with black feather centres that form long streaks along the back. The tail is cocked as it walks, exposing a single triangular panel of buffy-white feathers.

It favours shallow freshwater wetland habitats, such as *Phragmites* reedbeds, with margins of exposed mud or muddy breaks and dykes. It can adapt to smaller wetland habitats, provided cover is available, and wintering birds can be found on watercress beds, pools and ditches. In hard weather it may appear in atypical habitats and locations, even leaving cover to walk around on snow or ice in search of food. Although a bit of a rarity as a garden bird, it can appear in gardens that are undisturbed and close to its favoured wet habitats, particularly in the winter.

The most familiar call, usually heard coming from a dense reedbed, is a far-carrying 'pig squeal'. Typically of up to six notes, it is rather explosive in delivery and ranges from a hoarse and mournful groaning to a higher-pitched scream, descending and trailing off towards the end, as in "wheeah-wheeah-wheeah-wheeah-wheeoh…".

Hoopoe *Upupa epops*
Length: 26–28cm
Wingspan: 42–46cm

An unmistakable bird, with a startling pattern of large white spots and bands of white on black wings that give it the appearance of a huge butterfly when in flight. The tail is black with a broad white band. The head, neck and breast are pinky-buff, the belly white. The bill is rather long, slender and slightly decurved. It has long pinky-buff feathers on the crest, which are broadly tipped with black and, although usually lying flat to the head, are briefly raised vertically on alighting.

The Hoopoe is a scarce visitor to Britain from mainland Europe, usually appearing in southern counties as a spring 'overshoot'. It is typically found in open country habitats with scattered trees and bushes, farmland, orchards, vineyards, meadows, clearings and forest edge. It spends much of its time feeding on the ground, requiring a short sward of vegetation and open bare ground; for the very fortunate, it might just appear on a garden lawn!

The eponymous call of this lovely bird is the song of the male, a trisyllabic and hollow-sounding "wohp-wohp-wohp", "oop-oop-oop" or "woud'woud'woud!", somewhat like blowing across the top of a bottle. Repeated frequently and persistently, mainly during the breeding season, it sounds weak when close by but carries for quite a distance. Hoopoes also give a harsh and scolding "hwkhhhrrr" in alarm, and a less anxious-sounding, lower-pitched "khwrrrr".

Black Redstart *Phoenicurus ochruros*
Length: 13–14.5cm
Wingspan: 23–26cm

Similar in size and shape to the Common Redstart, it has an upright stance and a rusty-red tail that is habitually shivered. The male is charcoal-grey, with a blacker face and underparts, and a prominent white wing-patch on the secondaries, visible on the closed wing. The female is sooty grey-brown above and below, with a less obvious pale eye-ring than Common Redstart. In fresh plumage it shows fine silvery edges to the wing feathers.

Widespread and common on much of the Continent, in Britain it is a summer visitor with a small and localized breeding population, although a few birds overwinter in southern areas. It is a potential garden bird in certain inner cities and coastal ports, nesting on buildings, gasworks, industrial complexes and in marginal urban areas with rank weedy growths and cliff-like buildings that provide a facsimile of its original montane habitat.

The calls are similar to those of its close relatives, such as a high-pitched "seep" and a harder and 'stonier' "teck'teck'teck'teck", often combined into a "iisp'teck'teck'teck" when the bird is more anxious. The song is a rather high-pitched phrase, often sung at first light from a conspicuous high perch, introduced with a rattle of sweet notes followed by a curious quiet metallic scrunching and squishing noise, and then with a final flourish of three or four clearer rising notes, such as "eee'tyu'tyu'tyu'tyu. … .khxkhxkhxkhx tyu-che ch'chew".

Stonechat *Saxicola torquata*
Length: 11.5–13cm
Wingspan: 18–21cm

This small, compact and perky bird is usually seen perched prominently on the top of a bush or post, nervously flicking its wings and tail. The plumage of the male is rather striking, with a wholly black head and a prominent white half-collar that contrasts with both the dark upperparts and the deep orangey-rufous breast and flanks. It has a white band on the inner wing coverts that is often hidden at rest, the mantle is indistinctly streaked brown and blackish, and the rump is buffy and spotted black. Females are duller and browner with a dark-mottled throat.

Resident in western Europe, and favouring open country with low vegetation from uplands to plains, in Britain it is particularly attached to gorse thickets. It frequents heather, bracken, rough grassland, stony and sandy country, hillsides, cliffs and coastal areas, and is a potential garden visitor for those in rural or coastal areas. It may also be found more widely when dispersing in autumn and in winter.

The call is a dry 'chacking', typically repeated a number of times and often combined with a slightly upward-inflected "sweet" or "hweet", such as "tjak'tjak hweet"or "sweet tsac!'tsac!" . The song is short collection of rather feeble-sounding, high-pitched notes, rather monotonous and reminiscent of the song of the Dunnock, as in "sii'hew'ichi'hwee'tsiti'chwee'h u'wheet". It is usually delivered from the top of a bush or post, and occasionally in flight.

Sedge Warbler *Acrocephalus schoenobaenus*
Length: 11.5–13cm
Wingspan: 17–21cm

Firecrest *Regulus ignicapillus*
Length: 9–10cm
Wingspan: 13–16cm

A small brown-and-buff bird with a boldly marked head. Its broad buffish-white supercilium contrasts with a darker streaked crown, dark eyestripe and lores, and brown cheeks. The upperparts are brown with vague and diffuse streaking, the plain rump appearing brighter and warmer. The underparts are whitish with a buff wash on the breast and flanks, and juveniles have narrow dark streaks on the upper breast. It is often confiding, perching up on branches and reed stems.

This is one of our commoner summer migrant warblers, and a potential garden visitor to large and wild gardens that are close to its preferred habitats. It breeds in a wide variety of wetland habitats, favouring swampy bushy areas such as reedbeds with scattered bushes, tall rushes, riverside willows, canal sides and healthy ditches among arable crops, as well as drier places away from water, so long as there is lush herbage, such as hedges, overgrown meadows, coastal scrub and cereal crops.

It gives a grating nasal "chrrrrr" when anxious, and some scolding "tsuk" notes that are occasionally run together into a rattle when alarmed. The song is rather fast and vigorous, with abrupt changes across a wide tonal range. It comprises excited churring and harsh chattering notes, interspersed with high frequency trills and sweet whistles, and occasionally including mimicry of other songsters. It is a much more energetic sound when compared with the safe, pedestrian tempo of Reed Warbler's song, and is frequently given in song flights.

Of a similar size to the Goldcrest, but a shade more robust. Greener on the upperparts, it has a bold head pattern of a black-bordered yellow-orange crown stripe (brightest in the male), a broad white supercilium, a blackish line through the eye and a small whitish patch below the eye on a grey cheek. It has an orange-bronze collar patch on the side of the neck, and the wing is similarly patterned as on the Goldcrest.

It breeds across Europe in mixed and deciduous woodland, and also in parks, gardens and small wooded patches, usually with good undergrowth. It is less tied to conifers than the Goldcrest, although birds breeding in Britain tend to be in spruce or similar. A rare but possible visitor to gardens in Britain, where it is mainly an uncommon but regular migrant and winter visitor, with a small and localized breeding population in south-east England.

The song is sung by the male, and is a rapid repetition of a single high-pitched note, accelerating and rising in pitch, and becoming louder towards the end of the phrase, such as "sssi-zsi-zsi-zsi-zsi'zs'zs'zs'zs'zs'zs'zssi". It lacks the cyclical rhythm and terminal flourish present in the song of the Goldcrest, sounding fuller and less thin, even though it is of a similar frequency. The call note has a fuller and coarser quality than the Goldcrest's, with a quieter introductory note followed by three or four notes, such as zzi-ziii'zizizi".

Golden Oriole *Oriolus oriolus*
Length: 22–25cm
Wingspan: 44–47cm

Common Rosefinch *Carpodacus erythrinus*
Length: 13.5–15cm
Wingspan: 24–26.5cm

A truly exotic migrant visitor, but one that can turn up in gardens if the habitat is favourable. The male has a bright yellow body contrasting with black wings, tail and lores. It has yellow corners to the tail and a small yellow patch at the base of the primaries and the bill is red. The female is less bright, with yellow-green upperparts and wing coverts, blackish-grey wings and tail, and whitish, yellow-washed and streaked underparts.

A summer visitor found across most of mainland Europe, it is a scarce migrant to Britain, but small breeding colonies persist in south-east England, usually in commercial poplar plantations. Typical habitat is open deciduous woodland, particularly with mature trees, and they can be found in parks, large gardens, avenues, riverine woodland and shelter belts. Generally rather elusive, they stay high in the trees and are often seen only briefly, flying between gaps in the canopy.

This bird's presence is usually betrayed by its calls. The commonly heard call note is a harsh, nasal squawk, as in "arr'aa'arrhk", or a more insistent, emphatic "hrrrahhhk!". The eponymous 'O'ri'ole' song is a sweeter sound, a fluty and mellow yodelling whistle, typically of three or four overlapping notes with characteristic jumps in pitch, such as "hwi'loo'hweeo", "hwi'lli'oo'hweoo", " idlii'hweeeoo", a descending "hweedli'hwoh" and a shorter "hii'hweeoo".

A scarce but annual visitor to Britain, and one that may appear at bird feeders for the very fortunate! Often sluggish and unobtrusive, it is a thick-headed, swollen-billed bird with a longish cleft tail. The male is strongly coloured, with red on the head, throat, breast and rump, and a brown mantle and wings, the latter with pink-tinged wingbars. The females are rather demure, a nondescript grey-brown all over and paler on the underparts, which are streaked. The mantle is streaked and they show pale wingbars formed by pale tips to the wing coverts. Both sexes show a beady black eye. Juveniles are similar but somewhat more olive-toned, with bolder wingbars.

A summer visitor to Scandinavia and eastern Europe, wintering in south Asia, it is found in deciduous or mixed woodland clearings, forest edge, bushy thickets, damp meadows, willow scrub along watercourses and large parks. In Britain it is most frequent in autumn, when juveniles may appear in coastal areas, but occasional influxes in spring have led to the odd pair attempting to breed.

The call is an upwards-inflected "chuu'ih" or "shwe'eek", given at rest or in flight and reminiscent of one of the Greenfinch's calls. The song is a simple and pleasant cheery whistle of three to six syllables, commonly heard on the breeding grounds and sometimes described as 'pleased to meet you!' or more accurately as "ii'vhid ii'veiow", "seee to'whee'chew" or "chewee'wee'chu".

Index

Artwork Credits

Brin Edwards

Aquatic Warbler p5
Black Redstart p195l
Blackbird pp110b; 111b
Blackcap pp120; 121b
Black-headed Gull p52t
Blue Tit p140t
Brambling p172t
Bullfinch pp186b; 187
Carrion Crow p162t
Chaffinch pp170t; 171
Chiffchaff p129t
Coal Tit pp144; 145
Collared Dove p67
Common Cuckoo p73
Common Gull p54b
Common Rosefinch p197r
Common Whitethroat pp126;
   127t
Dunnock p106t
Fieldfare pp112t; 113
Firecrest p196r
Garden Warbler p123
Goldcrest p133
Golden Oriole p197l
Goldfinch p177
Great Spotted Woodpecker
   pp86t; 87
Great Tit p142
Green Woodpecker pp84t; 85
Greenfinch p174
Grey Heron pp32b; 33t
Grey Wagtail p99
Hawfinch pp188b; 189
Hoopoe p194r
House Martin pp94t; 95t
House Sparrow pp166b; 167b
Jackdaw p158
Jay pp5; 155
Kingfisher p82
Lesser Black-backed Gull p56

Lesser Spotted Woodpecker
   pp88; 89
Lesser Whitethroat p125
Linnet pp180; 181b
Long-tailed Tit p139t
Mallard pp26t; 27t
Marsh Tit p148
Meadow Pipit pp96t; 97
Mistle Thrush pp118b; 119
Nuthatch p150t
Pied Flycatcher p137
Pied Wagtail & White Wagtail
   pp100b; 101t
Redwing p117
Reed Bunting pp192t; 193
Robin pp3; 108t
Rook p161
Sedge Warbler p196l
Siskin pp178b; 179b
Skylark p90
Song Thrush pp11, 114; 115
Spotted Flycatcher p134t
Starling p164b
Stock Dove p63b
Stonechat p195r
Swallow p92
Tree Sparrow p168
Treecreeper pp152; 153
Turtle Dove pp68; 69b
Waxwing pp12, 102; 103
Willow Tit p146b
Woodpigeon pp64b; 65
Wren p104b
Yellowhammer p191

Mike Langman

Barn Owl pp74; 75
Blackbird pp17; 110t; 111t
Blackcap pp22; 121t
Black-headed Gull pp52b; 53
Blue Tit pp8; 140b; 141

Brambling pp172b; 173
Bullfinch p186t
Buzzard pp38; 39
Carrion Crow & Hooded Crow
   pp162b; 163
Chaffinch p170b
Chiffchaff pp128; 129b
Collared Dove p66
Common Crossbill pp184; 185
Common Cuckoo p72
Common Gull pp54t; 55
Common Whitethroat p127b
Dunnock pp9; 106b; 107
Fieldfare pp2; 112b
Garden Warbler p122
Goldcrest p132
Goldfinch p176
Great Spotted Woodpecker p86b
Great Tit pp1; 143
Green Woodpecker pp15; 84b
Greenfinch p175
Grey Heron p32t
Grey Wagtail p98
Hawfinch p188t
Herring Gull pp58; 59
Hobby pp42; 43
House Martin pp14; 94b; 95b
House Sparrow p166t
Jackdaw p159
Jay p154
Kestrel pp40; 41
Kingfisher pp13; 83
Lapwing pp48; 49
Lesser Black-backed Gull p57
Lesser Redpoll pp182; 183
Lesser Whitethroat p124
Linnet p181t
Little Owl pp76; 77
Long-tailed Tit pp138; 139b
Magpie pp156; 157
Mallard pp26b; 27b

Marsh Tit p149
Meadow Pipit p96b
Mistle Thrush p118t
Moorhen pp44; 45
Nuthatch pp7; 150b
Nuthatch p150b; 151
Oyster Catcher pp46; 47
Pheasant pp30; 31
Pied Flycatcher pp19; 136
Pied Wagtail & White Wagtail
   pp100t; 101b
Red Kite pp34; 35
Red-legged Partridge pp28; 29
Redwing pp20; 116
Reed Bunting p192b
Robin pp108b; 109
Rock Dove & Feral Pigeon pp60;
   61
Rook p160
Rose-ringed Parakeet pp70; 71
Siskin pp178t; 179t
Skylark p91
Sparrowhawk pp36; 37
Spotted Flycatcher pp16; 134b;
   135
Starling pp164t; 165
Stock Dove pp62; 63t
Swallow pp4; 93
Swift pp80; 81
Tawny Owl pp6, 78; 79
Tree Sparrow p169
Turtle Dove p69t
Water Rail p194l
Willow Tit pp146t; 147
Willow Warbler pp130; 131
Woodcock pp50; 51
Woodpigeon p64t
Wren pp10; 104t; 105
Yellowhammer p190